WOMEN WORKING IN SPORT

Timely, relevant and powerful. Jenny Coe and Dr Amy Whitehead have crafted an essential manual for Women Working in Sport, featuring contributions from guest authors who address breaking barriers through education, mentorship and allyship. The book offers practical solutions for achieving financial equality and ensuring women are valued equally in the sports industry workforce. It also tackles pressing issues like sexism and misogyny, urging a cultural shift in behaviour, particularly among men. This book is a guide for fostering awareness and understanding that what might be dismissed as 'banter' can significantly impact women's confidence. The sports industry should evaluate individuals based on work ethic, expertise, experience and passion, not gender.

~ Ed Bowers, Host of The Sports Career Podcast: Interviewed Over 400+ Sports Industry Professionals

Inspiring, insightful and thought-provoking. A book championing the untold stories of women working in sport, highlighting the power and incomparable potential of women's sport. A must read!

~ Emily Defroand, Football Communications Lead West Ham United, Former GB Hockey Player, Commonwealth Games and European Bronze Medallist

'Women Working in Sport' is a beautiful compilation of stories and experiences from brave, plucky and dedicated women working across a range of roles in sport. Sometimes you nod along, humbly identifying with their journeys; other times, you step back in sheer admiration. Their real-life anecdotes can both delight and hit like a sucker punch. None of these women should have had to be as thick-skinned as they are, but you're grateful that they were. They will act as a guide and inspiration for the next generation coming through.

~ Maggie Murphy, Co-Founder Equal Playing Field, Performance Consultant and Former CEO Lewes FC

WOMEN WORKING IN SPORT
SEE THEM, HEAR THEM, BE THEM

Jenny Coe and Dr. Amy Whitehead

Every possible effort has been made to ensure that the information contained in this book is accurate at the time of going to press. The publishers and author(s) cannot accept responsibility for any errors and omissions, however caused. No responsibility for loss or damage occasioned to any person acting, or refraining from action, as a result of the material contained in this publication can be accepted by the editor, the publisher or the author.

First published in 2025 by Sequoia Books

Apart from fair dealing for the purposes of research or private study, or criticism or review, as permitted under the Copyright, Designs and Patents act 1988, this publication may only be reproduced, stored or transmitted, in any form or by any means, with the prior permission in writing of the publisher, or in the case of reprographic reproduction in accordance with the terms and licenses issued by the CLA. Enquiries concerning reproduction outside these terms should be sent to the publisher using the details on the website www.sequoia-books.com

©Jenny Coe & Amy Whitehead 2025

The right of Carla Meijen to be identified as author of this work has been asserted in accordance with the Copyright, Designs and Patents act 1988.

ISBN
Print: 9781914110467
EPUB: 9781914110474

A CIP record for this book is available from the British Library

Library of Congress Cataloguing-In-Publication Data

Name: Jenny Coe & Amy Whitehead
Title: Women Working in Sport/Coe, Whitehead
Description: 1st Edition, Sequoia Books UK 2025
Print: 9781914110467
EPUB: 9781914110474

Print and Electronic production managed by Deanta Global Publishing Services, Chennai, India

Contents

Introduction: Breaking boundaries: Celebrating women
who transform sport 1
Jen Coe, Dr. Amy Whitehead, and a foreword from
Dr. Kristin McGinty-Minister

1. **The first but more to follow** 16
   Liz Mills
   FIBA - Afrobasket - Head Basketball Coach - Co-Founder
   Global Women in Basketball Coaching Network (Australia)

2. **'A sophomore mentality'** 27
   Kate Maher
   Senior Director Retail Innovation, Nike LAB &
   Jordan Distinction (Ireland & USA)

3. **Callary on coaching** 45
   Dr. Bettina Callary
   Canada Research Chair in Sport Coaching and
   Adult Learning, and Associate Professor (Canada)

4. **'Indian disability sport'**: Thriving through adversity 58
   Dr. Padmini Chennapragada
   Physical Design Engineer (India)

5. **Embrace the challenge** 67
   Dr. Danielle Prescott
   Talent Scout The FA / Associate dean postgraduate: Sports
   Coaching & Performance (UK)

6.	**'Key tools for life discipline & curiosity'** *Nadmina Skeff* *Head Football Coach Sfera Futebol Clube (Brazil)*	75
7.	**'It's all about the challenges you see, the mindsets and wardrobes you choose'** *Professor Stiliani 'Ani' Chroni* *Professor of Sport Psychology, Pedagogy, & Sport Coaching, and Sport Psychologist*	88
8.	**'Woman, life, freedom'** *Dr. Shakiba Moghadam* *Lecturer in Psychology, and Chartered Psychologist (UK)*	104
9.	**Acorns and oak trees** *Louisa Arnold* *Placement Advisor University of Kent (UK)*	118
10.	**'Remember that bravery is not the lack of fear but the ability to move forward in spite of fear'** *Paula Dunn MBE* *Head Coach UK Athletics (UK)*	126
11.	**'Develop enough courage so that you can stand up for yourself and then stand up for somebody else' –Maya Angelou** *Sarah Evans* *Membership manager - Leaders in Sport / Former GB Hockey Player (UK)*	137
12.	**'You can't play rugby, it's a boy's sport'** *Dr. Amy Whitehead* *Associate Professor of Sport Psychology and Coaching, and Sport Psychologist (UK)*	149
13.	**Questioning the Norms, Encouraging Change, and Strengthening the Path** *Jen Coe* *Performance Well-being-lead Women's Professional Football. Co-founder Impact the Game, High Performance Coach Developer (Ireland)*	160

14. **Sexisim in sport – smile more** 175
    Dr. Kristin McGinty-Minister
    Lecturer in Psychology - Manchester Metropolitan University,
    and Sport Psychologist (USA & UK)

15. **The ripple effect – the power of inspiring stories** 191
    Jen Coe, Dr. Amy Whitehead, and a foreword from
    Dr. Kristin McGinty-Minister

Introduction: Breaking boundaries

Celebrating women who transform sport

Jen Coe, Dr. Amy Whitehead, and a foreword from Dr. Kristin McGinty-Minister

INTRODUCTION

In the dynamic realm of sports, where grit, determination and excellence converge, a powerful force has long been overlooked and undervalued: women. For far too long, their stories, achievements and contributions have been overshadowed by the dominant narrative of their male counterparts or their confidence to own and celebrate them. But now, after years of countless interviews and impactful writing, this book unveils the remarkable chapters of women in sport – capturing their journeys, celebrating their triumphs and continuing to challenge the status quo.

Women often find themselves lagging behind in several critical areas. Despite their remarkable achievements and contributions, women's sports receive considerably less media coverage, perpetuating a cycle of invisibility that affects everything from sponsorship deals to recognition on the world stage. Furthermore, while women represent nearly 40% of sports participants globally, they hold only around 20% of leadership positions in sports organizations, limiting their influence in decision-making processes and hindering their ability to shape the direction of sports. In coaching, another critical area, women are vastly under-represented, comprising only about 28% of coaches globally, which not only perpetuates stereotypes but also limits opportunities for mentorship and guidance for athletes. Moreover, disparities in pay continue to persist, with female athletes often receiving substantially lower prize money, sponsorship deals and salaries compared to their male counterparts. These discrepancies extend to opportunities for participation, with barriers such as limited access to facilities and funding hindering the development of female athletes. Additionally, women are under-represented in sports governance bodies, meaning that their perspectives and interests may not be adequately considered in policy-making and resource allocation. Addressing these disparities requires a collective effort to promote gender equality and create more inclusive environments, ensuring that women have equal opportunities to excel in sports at all levels. Despite this, female athletes continue to excel and for the first time in Olympic history, we will now see gender parity (or almost, as there are still more men's events and medal opportunities for men). This is an increase of 6% in 12 years. There is more work to be done, more courageous conversations to be had and more agendas with diversity and inclusion on them.

With this in mind, and to provide context for the reader, Dr. Kristin McGinty-Minister provides below a short history of women's marginalization in sport and a lens into the recent backlash leveraged against women in sport. Following this, we detail the purpose and structure of this book.

DECENTRALIZING THE ISSUE OF GENDER INEQUITY IN SPORT AND BEYOND

As we develop as practitioners and people, we undoubtedly experience barriers that shape our development. Some of these experiences are relatively routine day-to-day stressors (e.g., difficulty scheduling life around busy sport schedules), others are substantial and individual (e.g., coping with loss), and some are common but less frequently spoken about – or even recognized (e.g., sexism). While many people find it relatively easier to talk about commonly identified experiences, those that might be conceptualized as 'taboo' by our culture (such as inequity) can be more difficult to discuss directly (e.g., BBC, n.d.). In regard to gender inequity, this presents a significant hurdle to progression on many levels. For example, if people are unaware of what gender inequity is, what it looks like in practice and that it is problematic, it becomes difficult to recognize and/or rectify. Additionally, if one cannot recognize symptoms of gender inequity (e.g., sexism) or why it occurs, it can be easy to assume that it is the fault of individuals or groups of women rather than a broader issue.

Centralizing women's maltreatment as their own fault can lead to ineffective coping mechanisms and fuel discourse that women who experience sexism 'deserve' it on some level, instead of problematizing the individuals and systems perpetuating sexism. Outside of the significant negative impact on the individual (e.g., compromised well-being for *everyone*; e.g., European Institute for Gender Equality, 2024), avoiding or ignoring these problems normalizes the experience; for example, many women share how sexism is a 'natural' barrier that they must work harder to overcome in sport because it is 'part of the culture' (e.g., Hindman & Walker, 2020; McGinty-Minister et al., 2024). However, gender inequity is not the fault of women, but a broader societal issue that is often supported and maintained by sport. Academics (e.g., Anderson, 2009; Connell, 1995) have long proposed that a primary driver of the development of sport was to maintain the patriarchal power structure in which we operate by allowing white, straight, 'able' men to demonstrate their 'innate' right to power through their physical prowess while also demonstrating that women, gender minorities and other groups do not possess the same; this was often accomplished through direct exclusion from sport and exercise.

This poses an important question: Is sexism indeed innate to sport culture? If so, *why* is this the case, and *what* can we do about it? This is a question we challenge the reader to explore throughout this book; more specifically, in this section of this chapter, I address these questions by first exploring the considerable link between sport and broader culture, and, more specifically, how sport has historically upheld (white, heteronormative and ableist) patriarchy. Throughout this book, we recognize the importance and significance of women's stories and their ability to communicate with one another as drivers of consequential change throughout history, and how we might apply this to sport culture to continue progressing with positive change.

Excluding women from sport to prevent broader progress

Even now, there is considerable discourse about the 'validity' of women's sport through topics surrounding women's bodies, the gender pay gap, viewership and allocated resources – as if a primary reason for the lack of space occupied by women in sport, and the 'slow' progression of women's sport, was not driven by active exclusion through policy and culture, often giving men's sport a significant head-start at pivotal periods in history. This is reflected in sports organizations today, where women's sport often occupies significantly less 'space'; in this regard, it would be applicable for organizations to reflect upon how the historical background of their sport and sport more broadly impact their current practices.

For example, in the 2023–2024 USA's NCAA Division One basketball season, Caitlin Clark (along with her talented teammates and competitors) shattered viewership records for both women and men (e.g., Romo, 2024). Following her draught to the WNBA's Indiana Fever, Clark's Fever jersey became the top-selling jersey of a professional basketball draught pick *of all time*, regardless of gender (Lenthang, 2024). The top pick of the (men's) NBA averages over ten million US dollars; despite Clark's record-breaking performance on the court, ability to attract novel and significant viewership to the game, and generating profit for numerous organizations through jersey and ticket sales, her salary equals 76,000 US dollars. While this *does* reflect the growth of the women's game with continued sustained viewership, multiple WNBA athletes have highlighted the inequity of their league(s). Kelsey Plum (of the Las Vegas Aces) corrects the 'misconception' that women 'want to be paid the same as LeBron' by stating that 'we're not asking to get paid what the men get paid …we're asking to get paid the same percentage of revenue shared', and continued by noting that women in the WNBA do not receive any percentage of jersey sales, unlike their NBA counterparts (The Residency Podcast). Importantly, while NBA athletes receive 50% of revenue share, WNBA athletes receive less than 10% (Darvin, 2024). This gap in interest, pay, and more between the NBA and WNBA is not happenstance but a result of targeted interventions to prevent women's progress more broadly.

Women were banned from countless sports in the early 1900s – a period defined by pushback by men in sport – with administrators, leaders and medical professionals proclaiming various physical and mental grounds for why women were unsuitable for sports (e.g., hysteria, running leading to damage to reproductive organs; Relentless, 2017). In the US, women were banned from college-level basketball in 1899, with some states making it illegal to play basketball in high school as well; the sport did not experience a true resurgence until the 1970s, after decades of women working to rectify the damage. Similarly, women in the United Kingdom have faced significant barriers in sports. One example is in football, where by 1921, there were around 150 women's football clubs in the United Kingdom – some matches drawing up to 45,000 spectators (e.g., the Football Association). However, driven significantly by men's resentment of the popularity of the women's game, women were banned from playing football from 1921 to 1970. Despite these barriers and the countless hurdles associated with the ban (e.g., lack of maternity rights and equal pay for professional women footballers), viewership of women's football has skyrocketed in the last several years.

While questioning the validity of women's place in sport is clear through their historical exclusion and current treatment, as outlined in several chapters in this book and in academic research, a poignant example of how women were barred from even casual sporting activities details how the exclusion of women from sport often had a greater, sociocultural purpose: preventing communication between women. When bicycles progressed in the late nineteenth century to have equal-sized wheels, they became a popular way to travel; they were much less work and much more (financially, physically) accessible than horses and carts and had the added benefit of not needing a man or two people to operate. As a result, there was a surge in women using bicycles to travel; women began communicating with women from other towns more frequently and in larger groups, leading to more discussions surrounding the early suffragette movement. Bicycles quickly became associated with the suffragette movement and the individuation of women more broadly, as women used them as vehicles to communicate with other women and/or attend protests. Horrifyingly to the men around them and society more broadly, some women began to prefer clothing that would make their cycling (and protesting) easier, such as shorter dresses or trousers. Picture the shock of onlookers in a society where women were generally confined to the home or escorted while in public (wearing modest clothing) upon seeing groups of women in trousers riding bicycles, with their suffragette signs hanging from the front, demanding women's right to participate in government.

INTRODUCTION 7

One magazine in 1896 stated: 'to men, the bicycle in the beginning was merely a new toy ... to women, it was a steed upon which they rode into a new world' (Stromberg, 2015). Subsequently, it did not take long for a resulting backlash in the form of a new 'women's disease' to strike the population and dominate the newspaper cycles for years: bicycle face. Male doctors argued that 'the unconscious effort to maintain one's balance produces a wearied and exhausted "bicycle face"', characterized by a clenched jaw, flushed expression and bulging eyes alongside other 'serious' medical concerns such as exertion of the lungs and heart (also known as general signs of exercise fatigue that could have been seen regardless of gender; Stromberg, 2015). The only manner of preventing or overcoming this condition was to avoid cycling entirely and return to being transported by horse and cart, which, of course, required a man or escort.

In a 2023 commencement speech at Smith University, CEO Reshma Saujani links bicycle face to modern-day imposter syndrome (Smith College, 2023). Oddly enough, 'imposter syndrome' is a term that first appeared to describe 'high achieving women' as the rise of women in the workforce surged (Rose & Imes, 1978). Saujani details how imposter syndrome demands that women fix themselves rather than look at the systems around them and notice what might need change. To stay quiet. One example of this in sport, mentioned earlier in this chapter, is the common assumption by women working in sport that it is a necessary hurdle to be overcome to have the privilege of occupying space in the sporting environment, rather than seeing this as a systemic issue. Her link demonstrates how bicycle face was never a women's problem, and neither is imposter syndrome or women's banning from sport. In other words, sexism is not an issue caused by women, nor is it our responsibility to live within the restricted confines that gender inequity attempts to enforce. These are mechanisms to keep women in the place that society deems fit for them to prevent disruption to the status quo.

Backlash to women's progress

Women have fought for centuries to progress to where we are today. Each surge forward in demonstrating women's competence and right to autonomy has resulted in societal backlash, especially in the form of professional and recreational sports, where men have historically reserved the 'right' to demonstrate their right to power. Those desiring the maintenance of a patriarchal structure have attempted to 'put women back in their place' by employing sexist assumptions about women's capacities: the early suffragette movement and bicycle face in the 1800s, actively banning women from sport in the 1900s as they began to compete with men's sports for popularity (Relentless, 2017), and in the 2000s, we have a less conspicuous form of exclusion of women from sport through sexism. For example, women working in sports, which is still largely occupied by men, are being excluded through sexism at interpersonal, organizational and cultural levels through intimidation and bullying, lack of maternity rights, policing gender stereotypes, denying career progression, harassment and more (e.g., McGinty-Minister et al., 2024; see Chapter 2). While the aforementioned barriers to women were indeed sexism, we did not have a word for the experience until the 1960s. Additionally, the 'outlet' of sexism has changed (e.g., indirect discrimination vs. outright banning of women in sports) due to the progression of policy and culture. Importantly, women's advancement in society has recently been met with an inevitable backlash as those who desire to maintain patriarchal power and privilege attempt to perpetuate and enforce what has been historically conceptualized as 'normal' (e.g., Grady, 2023; Faludi, 1991, Khan et al., 2023). For example, while young men have become more progressive in general, the single concept they have regressed in their opinions is gender roles, with younger men averaging less feminist than their fathers (e.g., Off et al., 2022; The Economist, 2024). A recent demonstration of this backlash and the key link between sport and society can be seen in a recent commencement speech at Benedictine College by Kansas City Chiefs kicker Harrison Butker. Butker employed the platform he obtained through his position in the American National Football League (partially attained by the privilege afforded to him by his mother, renowned physicist Elizabeth Butker) to inform the women *at their graduation* that they had been told a 'diabolical lie'. This lie, according to the kicker, was that having a career is meaningful for women; Butker followed this by declaring to these women, on the day they received degrees they had worked towards their entire lives, that their lives would not truly begin until they married and became homemakers. This sentiment accompanied various attacks on women's bodily autonomy and the LGBTQ+ community. While this was met with significant backlash worldwide, his speech resonated with many who would like to see women return to the kitchen, evidenced by Butker's jersey quickly selling out for the first time in his career (e.g., Liddell, 2024). While I initially felt 'bad' for the university having been 'tricked' into Butker's speech, then frustrated that they did not do their due diligence with their invited speaker, there is a significant chance that this was intentional. While universities in the US must demonstrate alignment with affirmative action policy, Benedictine College's statement about the incident calls the backlash to Butker's misogyny 'cancel culture' (Minnis, 2024). Many have hypothesized that this was a mechanism the university employed to portray the message being touted by current far-right extremism in the US that 'we *had* to let you earn your fancy degrees, now go follow your true vocation and support a man'.

However frustrating, modern-day sexism in sport is yet another function of *structural* gender inequity rather than a 'women's problem'. Just as bicycle face was not a mysterious illness that impacted only women, and women's reproductive organs do not malfunction if they run while playing basketball or football (e.g., Relentless, 2017), women are not incapable of working in sport. While there are numerous means by which women can keep fighting for, maintaining and progressing through their place in sport, we must decentralize sexism and gender inequity more broadly. This is not a *women's* problem, but society's problem, and in the present case, this is *sport's* problem.

MOVING FORWARD: PRIORITIZING WOMEN'S JOURNEY

Progressing women in sport

The aim of this book isn't just to spotlight the stats and stories but to support the continued development of environments that understand, recruit, retain and nourish the gender diversification of staff and all the benefits that come with that. In this book, we're offering a chance to explore some great work by excellent, thriving individuals as they bring new perspectives and greatness to the environments they work in and the legacy they leave when they create new moves in new spaces. These are the women lending a hand, hopping on Zoom calls to mentor future female coaches and paving the way.

In this era of heightened visibility for women working in sport, we find ourselves at a pivotal moment. The walls that once confined and constrained female athletes are crumbling (albeit slowly) and are being replaced by a growing chorus of voices demanding equal recognition and opportunities. The world is awakening to the realization that excellence knows no gender, and that the achievements of women in sport deserve not just respect but also celebration.

Various sports have made significant strides in celebrating gender equity, ensuring equal opportunities, representation and recognition for female athletes. Tennis, with tournaments like Wimbledon and the US Open, offers equal prize money for male and female competitors, elevating the status of women's tennis. Football (Soccer) has seen efforts by FIFA to promote gender equity, evident in the growing popularity and visibility of the FIFA Women's World Cup and by the Football Association in England, where the FA reported a surge in participation, bringing their number to 3.4 million women and girls playing football across the country. The WNBA (Women's National Basketball Association) players have consistently banded together to lead displays of collective activism addressing racism, policing, gender equality and more – and the league has never been more popular. Golf, through the LPGA (Ladies Professional Golf Association), offers substantial prize money and media coverage for female golfers. Track and field athletics, governed by World Athletics, ensure equal opportunities for male and female athletes in major events like the Olympics. Swimming, cycling and martial arts have also made strides in promoting gender equity. These examples showcase the positive impact of equal opportunities for female athletes in sports globally.

We have been blessed over the last few years with instrumental figures leaving ladders down, sharing tips and guidance through various mediums with a global audience. We want this book to disrupt thinking, be a vehicle for conversation and influence change. It brings awareness to some of the great shifts these brilliant women have been part of in their sporting space, some of them started with a single conversation. While it is essential to acknowledge the remarkable strides made by women themselves, it is equally important to highlight the role of their colleagues of all genders in supporting their journey and ambition. We frame this support not as a benevolent act, but as an awakened awareness – an understanding that empowering women working in sport benefits the entire athletic community.

GOALS OF THE BOOK

This book is a testament to the incredible individuals who have dedicated their lives to various aspects of sport. From athletes and coaches who have shattered records and ceilings and defied expectations to directors who have mentored and inspired, and from practitioners and academics who have championed equal representation to administrators who have paved the way for change – this collection of chapters showcases the brilliance and impact of women in the sports industry. Within these pages, you will find a diverse range of voices and perspectives, each contributing a unique lens to the narrative of women in sports. These contributors, experts in their respective fields, offer rich insights and experiences that illuminate the challenges faced, the victories achieved and the ongoing journey towards gender equality in sports.

This book explores a multitude of topics central to women in sports. We delve into the remarkable rise of female participation in traditionally male-dominated sports and sporting industries, the strides made in leadership roles and decision-making positions and the evolving portrayal of women in the media. We also examine the intersectionality of gender with race, ethnicity and other identities, exploring the experiences of women from diverse backgrounds.

The compilation of this book has been a labour of love, taking time to meticulously capture the journeys and stories of these remarkable women. It is through this comprehensive lens that we hope to provide a nuanced understanding of the challenges faced and the progress made.

The purpose of this book is not only to pay homage to the trailblazing women who have rewritten the rules and redefined what it means to stand on the shoulders of remarkable giants who came before to inspire future generations. By shedding light on their stories, we hope to empower those working in sport on and off the field, court, and pool, those working in strategic leadership roles and those who hold the decision-making power. We strive not just for equity and diversity to tick a box but to understand how to utilize this brilliance to achieve consistency in performance and well-being.

As you embark on this journey through the pages of this book, prepare to be inspired, educated and moved. You will engage with women who want you to dream, believe in your potential and pursue your passion for sports without limitations. The stories within will challenge perceptions, ignite discussions and leave a lasting impact. From the raw experiences shared by contributors to the value-stretching decisions they had to make, you will witness the resilience, determination and sheer brilliance of these women. They have overcome obstacles, shattered glass ceilings and blazed trails for future generations. Their stories are a testament to the power of perseverance, the importance of inclusive leadership and the gratitude for those strong leaders who gave them an equal chance.

Together, let us celebrate the extraordinary accomplishments of women working in sports and pave the way for a more inclusive and equitable future.

REFERENCES

Anderson, E. D. (2009). The maintenance of masculinity among the stakeholders of sport. Sport Management Review, 12(1), 3–14. https://doi.org/10.1016/j.smr.2008.09.003.

BBC. (n.d.). 100 Women, The Taboo of Feminism. https://www.bbc.co.uk/programmes/p04jqs44.

Clance, P. R., & Imes, S. A. (1978). The imposter phenomenon in high achieving women: Dynamics and therapeutic intervention. Psychotherapy, 15(3), 241–247. https://doi.org/10.1037/h0086006.

Connell, R. W. (1995). Politics of changing men. Radical Society, 25 (1), 135. https://www.proquest.com/openview/eb5ad73acbe66dcd01c0ffe4ff500286/.

Darvin, L. (April 24, 2024). Caitlin Clark's move to the WNBA illuminates pay inequities. Forbes. https://www.forbes.com/sites/lindseyedarvin/2024/04/23/rising-wnba-stars-illuminate-inequities-and-spark-new-calls-for-change/.

European Institute for Gender Equality. (July 17, 2024). What Is the Impact of Sexism at Work? https://eige.europa.eu/publications-resources/toolkits-guides/sexism-at-work-handbook/part-1-understand/what-impact-sexism-work?language_content_entity=en#:~:text=Sexist%20expectations%20and%20behaviour%20have,harassment%5B3%5D%5B4%5D.

Faludi, S. (1991). Backlash: The Undeclared War Against American Women. New York: Three Rivers Press.

Grady, C. (February 3, 2023). The mounting, undeniable Me Too backlash. Vox. https://www.vox.com/culture/23581859/me-too-backlash-susan-faludi-weinstein-roe-dobbs-depp-heard.

Hindman, L. C., & Walker, N. A. (2020). Sexism in professional sports: How women managers experience and survive sport organizational culture. Journal of Sport Management, 34(1), 64–76. https://doi.org/10.1123/jsm.2018-0331.

Khan, A., Tant, E., Harper, C., & Align Platform. (2023). Facing the Backlash: What Is Fuelling Anti-Feminist and Anti-Democratic Forces? https://www.alignplatform.org/sites/default/files/2024-03/align-framingpaper-backlash-mar24-es.pdf.

Lenthang, M. (April 17, 2024). Caitlin Clark's popularity intensifies after WNBA draft. NBC News. https://www.nbcnews.com/news/sports/caitlin-clarks-indiana-fever-jersey-becomes-top-selling-jersey-draft-p-rcna148226.

Liddell, J. (May 17, 2024). Harrison Butker NFL jersey sales are up in aftermath of controversial commencement speech. The Independent. https://www.independent.co.uk/news/world/americas/harrison-butker-jersey-nfl-chiefs-b2546980.html.

McGinty-Minister, K. L., Swettenham, L., Champ, F. M., & Whitehead, A. E. (2024). 'Smile more': women's experiences of sexism while working in sport from a socio-ecological perspective. Sport in Society, 1–24. https://doi.org/10.1080/17430437.2024.2321357.

Minnis, S. D. (June 17, 2024). We invited Harrison Butker to speak at our college. We won't bow to cancel culture. USA Today. https://eu.usatoday.com/story/opinion/2024/06/17/harrison-butker-speech-benedictine-college-cancel-culture/74083499007/.

Off, G., Charron, N., & Alexander, A. (2022). Who perceives women's rights as threatening to men and boys? Explaining modern sexism among young men in Europe. Frontiers in Political Science, 4. https://doi.org/10.3389/fpos.2022.909811.

Relentless. (August 10, 2017). To be a female athlete: The history of defiance (Part 1: 1800–1969). Relentless21. https://relentless21.wordpress.com/2017/08/01/to-be-a-female-athlete-the-history-of-defiance-part-1-1800-1969/.

Romo, V. (April 10, 2024). Women's NCAA championship TV ratings crush the men's competition. NPR. https://www.npr.org/2024/04/10/1243801501/womens-ncaa-championship-tv-ratings#:~:text=with%20Rachel%20Martin-,Women's%20NCAA%20championship%20draws%20a%20record%20number%20of%20TV%20viewers,watched%20basketball%20game%20since%202019.

Smith College. (June 20, 2023). Imposter Syndrome Is a Scheme: Reshma Saujani's Smith College commencement address[Video]. YouTube. https://www.youtube.com/watch?v=BoHDDgeQtIc.

Stromberg, J. (March 24, 2015). "Bicycle face": A 19th-century health problem made up to scare women away from biking. Vox. https://www.vox.com/2014/7/8/5880931/the-19th-century-health-scare-that-told-women-to-worry-about-bicycle.

The Economist. (March 13, 2024). Why young men and women are drifting apart. The Economist. https://www.economist.com/international/2024/03/13/why-the-growing-gulf-between-young-men-and-women.

The Football Association. (n.d.). Kicking Down Barriers. www.thefa.com. https://www.thefa.com/womens-girls-football/heritage/kicking-down-barriers.

The Residency Podcast. (November 24, 2022). EP. 122 - Kelsey Plum Exposes How Underpaid Wnba Players Really Are!! [Video]. YouTube. https://www.youtube.com/watch?v=sF3wRIublJ0.

CHAPTER 1
The first but more to follow

Liz Mills

Since 2021, I've been interviewed by the BBC, the Associated Press, CNN and ESPN numerous times. In the past 2 years, I've completed over 50 interviews, podcasts and panels. Since arriving back from my season in Cote d'Ivoire, on average, I've been doing four interviews or podcasts a week. Why have I been asked to do all of the above? The answer is simple: I am part of a small subset of women who have become 'the first' to achieve a feat no other woman has accomplished before me. I consider myself an ambassador when it comes to women in sport and discussions around diversity, equality and inclusion in the sport industry. My name is Coach Liz Mills, and I am currently the head coach of the senior men's club team Abidjan Basketball Club (ABC) in Abidjan, Cote d'Ivoire (Ivory Coast). With over 20 years of coaching experience, I have spent the last 12 years coaching men's basketball in Africa. I have been a head coach and assistant coach of men's club teams and national teams in Zambia, Cameroon, Rwanda, Kenya, Morocco and now Cote d'Ivoire. I am the first female head coach to lead a men's national team at a FIBA continental championship (AfroBasket, 2021), the first woman to coach a men's club team in Morocco (thus becoming the first female to coach a men's team in the Arab world) and the first female head coach in the NBA/FIBA Basketball Africa League (2022).

My coaching journey started in Sydney, Australia, where I was born and raised alongside my identical twin sister, Vic. Being an identical twin is a crucial part of who I am; I do not know what it's like to consider myself as just an individual. I didn't learn to say 'I' until I went to university. Up until then, it was always 'we', and this has laid the foundation for my ability to be part of and lead teams. Our parents, Robyn and Don Mills, encouraged us from an early age to play a variety of sports, as well as excel in other areas such as academics, art and music. This allowed us to have a very well-rounded education and helped create a wide perspective. As we were playing multiple sports, we also enjoyed watching the Australian Netball League on the ABC (Australian Broadcasting Corporation). Watching these amazing athletes influenced our goal of wanting to be netball superstars when we grew up. It was only by chance that at the age of 10, we tuned in to watch the ABC, and the Women's National Basketball League (WNBL) was being shown. We were instantly hooked! At the time, some of Australia's greatest players were entering the league, such as Lauren Jackson and Penny Taylor, and what was even more impactful was the number of female head coaches marching up and down the sidelines. Just to see such a plethora of intelligent, strong and successful female coaches was empowering and inspiring. As a young girl, watching Coach Carrie Graf win numerous WNBL titles with the Canberra Capitals planted a seed in my mind that would eventually sprout into my decision to become a basketball coach. Having role models such as Coach Graf reinforces the notion that you can be it if you can see it and is a huge reason as to why I continue to try and be visible to as many young girls and women as possible across the world. You never know who you are inspiring and how much of an impact you can have just on one person.

Having been inspired by the female coaches in the WNBL, I decided that I wanted to coach. I was realistic about my abilities as a player but knew that I had leadership capabilities that would translate to coaching. My sister and I had previously coached netball, and at the age of 16, we started to coach basketball at the miniball level (U8s) while we were still in high school. There were no undergraduate coaching courses at the time, so for university I studied sport science and sports management and then later went on to study for my master's in education, majoring in coaching. I knew being highly qualified would also help me have a competitive advantage over my male colleagues, so I was very strategic about my university and post-university education. During this time, my sister and I continued to be head coach and assistant coach at the junior club and representative level, with my final year coaching in Australia being with an Under 21 women's representative team in Sydney, Australia.

I wouldn't be where I am today without Heroes Play United. In 2011, this club team in Zambia gave me my first opportunity to coach a men's team. As a woman in sport, you expect to come across hurdles, resistance, ageism and sexism. These are unfortunate facts in our reality as women in this industry. Growing up in Australia, it was clear that unless I wanted to coach juniors (and predominantly girls) or women, I would never be a head coach for a men's team at the highest level. There were no women head coaches, let alone assistant coaches, in the NBL or at the national team level anywhere in the world. So when my friend invited me to watch the pre-season tournament of the men's national league in Zambia, I had no thoughts about going there to try and find a team to coach. I was there as a spectator/fan. The games were fun and exciting to watch, and after a while I thought to myself, 'I could definitely coach here.' So, I took a gamble and approached one of the teams – Heroes Play United. I was very fortunate in that the team was managed by Maziko Phiri, who had spent a lot of time overseas working in international organizations, and he was very open minded. He saw me as an experienced coach from Australia, not a 'female' coach. He agreed to let me coach one practice session with the team, and this turned into me being invited back the next day and then being asked to be head coach for the rest of the season. We ended up winning the national championship, after the team had not won the title in eight years. What I will always cherish most about this team was its underdog mentality and the complete belief that we could beat anyone and win the title against all odds. Without this experience and championship, I may not have decided to continue coaching in Africa.

Throughout my coaching career in Africa, I have never had an agent. I have always found ways to create opportunities to coach. Except for one team, I have approached or put myself in a position to be hired by a club or a national team. As a woman in this industry, I have always understood that it will only be in very rare circumstances that we are going to be tapped on the shoulder and handed a job. As a solution to this, I have created my own opportunities, and I encourage other coaches and women in other areas of our ecosystem to do the same. For example, in 2018, I flew to Tunis, Tunisia, during the 2019 FIBA World Cup African Qualifiers. Armed with my printed-out scouting reports, advanced stats and previous experience coaching in Africa, I approached the national team coaches working at the tournament and as a result became assistant coach for the Cameroon men's team for the next window of the qualifiers. In 2022, I went to the BAL Qualifiers in Abidjan, Côte d'Ivoire, spoke to a few different club presidents and as a result, was offered the head coaching job of Abidjan Basketball Club. Be brave enough to create your own opportunities. Be brave enough to try, and most importantly, be brave enough to fail. No doubt there will be rejections, but you never know if you don't ask. The worst thing someone can say to you is 'no'. All this means is that this wasn't the opportunity for you and that you need to go out and continue to knock on or create doors for you to go through.

Looking back over my coaching career, I've had numerous highs and lows. The successes have allowed me to promote my views on gender equality, diversity and inclusion in sport, and my lows have given me opportunities for personal and professional growth and development. My proudest achievement as a coach was working with the Kenyan men's national team and helping them qualify for the 2021 AfroBasket for the first time in 28 years. We managed to beat 11-time AfroBasket champions Angola by 1 point on the buzzer to qualify. After a decade of coaching in Africa, being able to beat a team like Angola was a moment I will treasure. No words can describe the euphoria I felt and how important that moment was for the history of basketball in Kenya. It was also an important moment for female coaches in men's basketball. It was the first time a female coach had led a team to qualify for one of FIBA's continental championships, and later that year I became the first female head coach of a men's national team at any FIBA continental championship (AfroBasket, 2021). I became an 'overnight' success, but more importantly, it allowed me to shine a spotlight on female coaches in our sport. It created dialogue around diversity, inclusion and equality. It also revealed how much work our sports journalists need to do to also help promote equality. Too often, gender was the entire focus rather than my ability to coach and the great relationships I built with players. I'm a great 'female coach', as opposed to just being a great coach. Word choice or the use of emotive language to help make me sound more 'feminine' to the readers was also employed a number of times, especially by male journalists. I've been able to speak to these journalists after articles have been published and helped them understand why word choice and the messaging need to be something they consider more highly moving forward.

My greatest challenge as a coach was in 2017 in Lusaka, Zambia. After coaching in the country on and off for almost six years and winning two national men's titles as head coach for two different club teams and leading the men's national university team to their best results at the Southern African and All-African University games, I was appointed assistant coach, *not* head coach, for the men's national team. While upset and frustrated that I was appointed assistant, I was told the federation felt it would be better for the national team to be coached by a Zambian, hence the choice of the head coach (who happened to be male). Though, in reality, I knew the head coach would be unable to attend 90% of practices (due to his work commitments), which meant I had full reign anyway, the title grated. However, I had grown too comfortable in my time in Zambia and overconfident, and when the team failed to qualify for the 2017 FIBA AfroBasket, I was devastated. I really felt that I could be the driving force for this team to qualify. After the tournament, I returned to Australia and even considered giving up coaching. I have my sister Vic, friends and parents to thank for picking me up out of a deep depression and encouraging me to keep going. This reality check was exactly what I needed. In Zambia, I had become a big fish in a small pond. Too often, as coaches, we get too comfortable coaching at our clubs, or in our cities and states. Comfort stifles growth. In the harsh light of reality and looking straight in the mirror, I was able to critically assess my own performance and take accountability for the things I had done that contributed to our performance. The ability to self-assess as objectively as possible is a key factor that separates average coaches from good coaches. Without this challenging experience, I wouldn't be the coach I am today. It inspired me to continue developing as a coach, as well as acquire new skills (film and analytics). It also led me to make the tough decision to leave Zambia and continue my coaching journey in another African country. If Zambia had qualified in 2017, I probably would have continued to coach there and perhaps never achieved the other accolades I have or been able to raise awareness for female coaches.

Throughout most of my career, I have felt like the sole survivor on an island. I have had no other women to chart the way for me to follow or to seek mentorship from. This is why men have had the greatest influence on my coaching career. From the male coach who initially encouraged Vic and me to start coaching basketball at 16, to Maziko Phiri (general manager of Heroes Play United) in Lusaka, who gave me my first chance to coach a men's team in Africa, and the other great male mentors I've had along the way. Coach John Zimba was a mentor for me during my time in Zambia and really helped me navigate the different culture of the country and style of basketball, without making me feel less because I was a woman. Coach Rex Nottage in Sydney was a mentor for me when I returned to Sydney in 2013 to complete my master's degree in coaching. He was one of the only coaches in Australia to understand the value of my time coaching in Africa rather than looking down on the experience. Kita Thierry from Congo (managing director of NBA Africa) has been with me since 2012 and regardless of where I have coached in Africa, has always been in the background ready to offer a hand, an ear or advice. I was inspired by women to coach, but I have been mentored by men. This feeling of isolation led me to go in search of other female coaches working with men's teams, as well as any female coaches working in professional/elite basketball. Too often, we try to join the 'boys club' in basketball and try to fit into the toxic masculine culture of our sport. Understanding that there are so many female coaches out there who feel isolated or need female mentorship, my twin sister and I created the 'Global Women in Basketball Coaching Network'. The network is the first international network for female basketball coaches. The mission of the network is to connect female coaches from around the world on a platform where they can engage, empower and elevate each other to success. The network aims to build a safe environment for a diverse and inclusive community of female coaches. This network has allowed me to connect with so many female coaches from around the world and to also help mentor the next generation of female coaches.

I've also had the privilege to coach some of the greatest players in Africa who have been advocates for me in my career not only in Africa but also outside the continent. One of the greatest joys of working with adults is the bonds of friendship you can form off the court. I have been lucky throughout my time in Africa to call many of my former players friends, such as Chongo Chona from Zambia, Tuna Amutenya from Namibia, Kenny Gasana from Rwanda, Tylor Ongwae from Kenya and Abdoulaye Harouna Amadou from Niger. When I was coaching AS Sale in Morocco, I was without an assistant coach and living in my first North African Muslim country. Harouna took me under his wing, making sure I was settled in Rabat and helping me understand the culture and religion of the country. He was also a great support at practice, helping with translation and serving as a sounding board for basketball ideas. What would be the most unpleasant and challenging coaching season of my career was made bearable because of Harouna. He has since joined me at Abidjan Basketball Club in Cote d'Ivoire, for the Basketball Africa League. While this kind of collaboration may be uncommon, I think that's the advantage of working with adults. Players come with their own valuable experiences, and I have always found the process of collaboration very rewarding and successful for both parties.

How have I overcome the challenges and hurdles throughout my career? I wish there was a magic answer to this question that we could all follow, but unfortunately each situation presents its own unique challenges. I do, however, hope that my following advice may be of use to you on your journey. For me, the keys to my success have been these five factors: having a deep sense of purpose, having a growth mindset, being highly prepared, being resilient and creating my own opportunities. I have always worked towards goals, and part of that journey is understanding that there will be obstacles and hurdles in the way (nothing worth having comes easily). It is important to remember to keep your focus on the goal and not be distracted by these hurdles. An example would be when I dealt with sexism. When I was in Cameroon for the 2021 AfroBasket Qualifiers with the Kenyan national team, I went to put my bag down on the head coach's chair on the bench. A female official from the bench hurried over and told me that I had put my bag down on the head coach's chair and then pointed at our male assistant coach, assuming that he must be the head coach. I told her no, I was the head coach, and then proceeded to help Kenya qualify for AfroBasket. I did not let this incident, which has been common throughout my career, distract me from my goal and the team's goal. After the tournament, she apologized profusely and said she was so happy and inspired to see a woman in my position. By being a visible role model, I am slowly changing mindsets. People have to see it to challenge the status quo. As previously mentioned, my experiences in Zambia helped change my mindset towards a growth mentality. When you're constantly challenging yourself to improve and build your coaching skills, it's hard to be overlooked. I have an undergraduate degree, a master's degree, several diplomas and have attended countless clinics. It's hard to argue that many of my male counterparts are as 'qualified' as me. This has helped give me an edge over some other coaches throughout my career.

Women, without fail, have to go above and beyond to prove their worth. You will always have to be 'more'. This is why I make sure I am as prepared as possible whenever I join a new club or national team. I make sure I research the country in terms of its history, culture and religion, and I do as much research on the players and team as possible. At the first practice, I want to be able to greet every player by name and already be able to discuss their position and skill set. This is a great way to start building a positive relationship with players and for them to see that you are prepared and ready to go. Due to the number of years I have now spent coaching in Africa, my expertise is sought across the continent, and I'm often asked to consult for other teams and federations. Players from across the continent reach out to me, including players I've never even coached. They know that I have put in the time and effort to know the domestic leagues, continental championships and national tournaments, and through my expansive network, I am usually the 'first in the know'! This has also helped create an image of hard work and preparedness that no other coach has in Africa. This has become my competitive advantage.

There have been many times throughout my coaching career in Australia and Africa where I have faced discrimination and failure. These could have given me numerous reasons to quit and try another career. That is why resilience has been key to my ability to continue into uncharted territory and prove that women can be successful at the highest levels of basketball. I understand that I not only represent myself but am judged as representing all female coaches. How I behave, what I say and my success or failure on the court reflect on women as a whole. That is why I take being a role model very seriously and understand that I am leading the way for female coaches in FIBA basketball. If I have to take some hits along the way so that women behind me have an easier journey, I am prepared to do that. This also ties into my deep sense of purpose in what I am doing. I strongly believe in promoting equality and equity in our sport, and by leading by example, I hope to change minds and inspire other female coaches on their own journeys to success.

Ubuntu is an African philosophy that means 'I am because we are'. Essentially, I can only be all I can be if you are all you can be. I know without a doubt I would not be where I am today without my twin sister, family, friends and the teams I have worked with. This African philosophy has not only shaped me as a person but as a coach, forming the foundation of my coaching philosophy. The most valuable lesson I have learnt in my career is to have perspective. I understand the privilege I have to be able to coach basketball and recognize that in the grand scheme of things, winning or losing is not comparable to those in positions regarding global security, saving lives or solving world peace. It also allows me to value the human side of players. Who are they as people away from basketball? When players understand that you care more about them as a person, as opposed to what they can do for you as a player, this builds a more positive and productive relationship. It also ties into Ubuntu. As a coach, my job is to develop players but also human beings. These people will also challenge you as a coach and a person and as a result, hopefully, both parties will grow and develop into being better people, players and coaches.

My coaching goal is to be the first woman to head coach a men's national team at a FIBA World Cup or the Olympics. I like chasing 'firsts'. It keeps me motivated, especially in proving to people that women can succeed in coaching men's basketball. I want to continue to shine a spotlight on the inequality that exists at all levels within our sport and to influence federations to adopt more inclusive and diverse selection policies with regard to coaches and female participation in our sport. I want to continue to develop as a coach during this time, and once I have achieved my goal of coaching at an Olympics or a World Cup, I will retire. Being a woman of many firsts has taken a physical and emotional toll, and I would like the next chapter of my life to involve mentoring coaches and being on the administration side of basketball. I would also like to continue to promote female coaches, especially through the Global Women in Basketball Coaching Network.

If I could travel back in time, I would encourage my younger self to believe that I could be and do anything I set my mind to. I would also tell my younger self that success is a concept that only you can determine. Success looks different to every individual. Don't let others define it for you. There are many different paths to success, and as you constantly evolve as a person, goals will too. It's okay to change your mind, and it's ok to change your path. Be flexible and open-minded. There is no single path to success.

CHAPTER 2
'A sophomore mentality'

Kate Maher

A sophomore is a widely used term for a student in their second year of education, typically in an American university. I went to an American university, and I was a sophomore. At the time I was curious as to why this strange word was used. I looked it up then, and for the purpose of this chapter, I looked it up again:

> 'It comes from the Greek word "Sophos", meaning clever or wise', said Sokolowski. 'And the word "Moros"', meaning foolish. And so sophy moore – or sophomore – means 'a wise fool'.

That 'soph' also appears in the word 'philosophy', which means a love of wisdom. And that same root word 'moros' gives us the word 'moron'.

This description both made me laugh and reinforced the point I am attempting to make in this chapter.

Having spent eight years in the American education system, I quite like the thought of maintaining a sophomore mentality ever since being an actual sophomore. Twice. In my case, I noticed a distinct shift in my perspective from my freshman to my sophomore year: I felt a little more seasoned than my rookie year – less of a headless chicken or a deer caught in the headlights, as the cliches go. As a sophomore, you've likely learnt some lessons, made some mistakes and you're still trying to prove yourself. You're no longer able to play the newbie card, and you can't be complacent, or you'll be overtaken and passed over by someone else. You have to practise and prepare and stay ready for your opportunity, and when it comes, you have to grab it, trust your training and get out there and perform. You're on the cusp of success, but also on the cusp of failure. It's like halftime of a match. Anything is possible, and it can still go either way. You may be down, but there's still a chance. You may be up, but you can't take it easy. It is literally a metaphor for life, and this is how I feel most of the time, in life and in work.

My rookie year, in contrast, was fraught with expectations and self-identity issues; I was constantly asking myself, 'Should I be here? Am I good enough? Was this a big mistake? Am I actually good enough to have earned this spot on the team?' These questions were complemented by a barrage of doubts and negative affirmations you tell yourself: saying things like 'I'm never going to figure this out', or 'I thought this was going to be so much different', or 'the coach doesn't like me anymore'. I would love to say this was just me and my own naïveté, but I've learnt that many rookies experience something similar. The leap from high school to college is a big one in so many ways beyond leaving home and taking your first baby steps into adulthood. You see, to become a rookie on a Division 1 Women's basketball team, you have to have been a solid high school prospect. You have to have been seen as able to add value to a university team, and you most likely stood out from the local competition in a way that got the attention of college coaches. The process is one of recruitment, where the coach pursues you, tells you how much they like your style of play, tells you how great you are and how great you can be. They tell you how much value you can add to their team, promising nothing but great experiences, successes, growth, development and ideally championships along the way. A dream, right? Not for long. For most rookies, things just don't turn out that way. Your rookie year can involve a lot of 'doing your time', 'learning the ropes' – all the cliché sayings for proving your value. It's tough to earn minutes on the roster no matter how hard you practise and how well you learn the plays. You have to earn your spot, and that usually means beating out someone more senior than you for theirs. And for the life of them, they do not want to see that happen. Yes, they are your teammates, but you are their competition. I have had the exact same feelings every time I've started a new job. I've had it at ASICS, at Adidas, at Gensler and at Nike. It's wild – you would think I would've outgrown this by now, but it's not just about me and my comfort or confidence level. It is partially expected and partially an environmental shift in context. You're part of a new team, and it takes time to both acclimate and be accepted.

Sophomore year, though, the year after that rookie year of disillusionment, is a real sink or swim situation. There are new rookies now, and so you either step up and show them and the coaches that you've got things figured out or you don't. It can only go one of three ways from there: (1) You see it for what it is, take assertive action and ask, 'Why not me?' You start proving yourself and, in turn earn playing time. (2) You acclimate too slowly and possibly never or rarely make it off the bench. Or (3) You quit. It sounds bad, but it happens more than one would think. It's not something you ever envisioned for yourself, but in that tough environment, quitting is tempting. When that alarm goes off at 5:15 a.m., and you wake up fatigued, bruised and sore from the mental and physical battles of the day before, and you have to head to the gym for the first of three workouts that day, quitting is tempting. When the coach has you running full-court sprints 30 minutes after your 3-hour practice was due to finish, quitting is very tempting. At your lowest moments, and when it just feels like nothing is going your way, the impulse to quit is at its strongest. And as luck would have it, you're at your weakest, not a great combination. So you need something to combat that impulse to quit, and it had better be gladiator strong. You need to dig deep and find motivation. More accurately, you need to find *your* motivation. You need to call on it and harness it to give you all the strength you need to say no to quitting and say yes to succeeding.

Ironically, and shamefully, my motivation comes from quitting. I am not really a quitter. I say not really because I cannot say it explicitly due to that one pivotal time when I did quit. I think that's the reason I can never quit again and haven't quit since.

A LITTLE ABOUT ME

But before I get into my quitting story, I should probably tell you a little about me. My name is Kate Maher. I'm the fourth of six rowdy kids, born in the 1980s to two young parents living in the countryside in the southeast of Ireland. I am currently working in my dream job, at what is commonly known as the best sports brand in the world, Nike. As you will learn more about me in this chapter, you will come to understand the cornerstones of my passion and my purpose: the importance of sports (duh), design, travel, teamwork and, of course, sneakers. I've worked in the sports industry for over 12 years now, with time spent at ASICS, Adidas, Jordan and now Nike. I love my job, and it is truly my dream role, where my team get to imagine, design and create the global store portfolios, and I am keenly aware that I am privileged to occupy it at this point in time. That said, at the heart of it all I'm just an Irish kid with a deep desire to make the most of my opportunities, with a genuine love for sports and specifically basketball. I'm also a kid whose life has been fuelled and dramatically changed for the good by the power of sports. Sport has given me lifelong friends, mentors and even a first-rate education. It has allowed me to travel the world. It has taught me both confidence and humility. Sport has unequivocally changed my life.

QUITTING

So back to the quitting incident: an inflection point and a moment that changed me in a way that still has a lasting impact today. We need to rewind back to when I was about 11 years old. Surprisingly, it was a pretty mild and dry day in mid-summer. I say surprisingly because I grew up in

Ireland, and it was rarely mild and dry day in mid-summer. The quitting incident took place at our local GAA (Gaelic Athletic Association) pitch. The referee blew the halftime whistle, and all 15 of us plodded over to the sideline to our coach (the local water plant superintendent, moonlighting as a volunteer coach). We were down by a lot, and I was particularly upset by the 'unfairness' of what was happening on the pitch. The 'unfairness' I refer to was the cumulative result of three things: (1) We were getting thrashed by our opponents (might I add we were mostly under-14s playing in an under-16s match). (2) My younger sister was in goal and had already let in an untold number of goals at this point (we still dispute how many to this day). And (3) I was getting absolutely manhandled, and in my opinion viciously fouled by a wild 14-year-old townie from the notorious St. Saviors Club (whoever thought it was a good idea to give this wildling a wooden stick to swing around was beyond me).

To give you a bit of context here, we were playing the Irish sport of hurling, more locally known as Camogie when played by female athletes. I know we are just meant to say athletes now as we become more progressive with our language, but the fact remains that gender distinction and legacy still have not evolved in all corners of the world, and the balancing act of tradition and progress is seen here too. As mentioned, I was about 11 and my sister was around 9, and we were called up to play on the Under-16 ladies' team due to a shortage of available players. (Come to think of it, it was probably something to do with it being a mild dry day in summer and the absent teenage girls were undoubtedly lured to hang around the beach – a rarity indeed.) Now to be fair to us (and so that our poor coach isn't deemed unreliable when it comes to child welfare in sport), it was the early 1990s, coaches' training likely didn't exist, and both my sister and I were fairly athletic kids (having two older brothers and about a million cousins). By that, I mean we could well handle ourselves at U-12 and even do okay at U-14s. We'll agree to say that us playing U-16 must've been a pretty desperate situation. Anyway, after arriving on the sideline, I was all worked up and I complained to my coach about this 'unfairness', to which he paid no heed nor displayed even a shred of sympathy for my cause. I told him how I was being elbowed in the ribs and slapped across my shins, but still no ounce of sympathy was shown. I couldn't believe it. I saw red, and well, I lost it. I threw a humiliating tantrum on the sideline, ripped off my skirt (I was wearing shorts underneath – don't worry), and I declared that I wasn't playing anymore. To emphasize my point even further, I stormed over to my grandmother's car, which was conveniently parked just beyond the sideline of the pitch, and I plonked myself down in the front seat, arms aggressively folded, and stared straight ahead. I was proud of myself for sticking up for myself, and asserting my independence, and for having the actual gall to walk off the pitch. I was emboldened by a deadly combination of rage and pride. The feeling was glorious. And fleeting. It lasted for what I can only calculate as a grand total of approximately five seconds. As soon as I got to the car, I had a new opponent: my grandmother. She asked what I was doing in the car and dutifully heard me out as I explained the injustices and the 'unfairnesses'. As I unloaded a second time, it all started to sound a tad on the dramatic side, even to me. But I was steadfast. Sure, wasn't I justified in my complaints? It was still halftime, and she suggested that I take a minute to cool off and then go back over to join my team, still huddled on the sideline. I was having none of it, and I outright refused.

Being a blood relative of mine, she, of course, wasn't satisfied with failing to persuade me. She had no choice but to change tactics and take on the whole grandmother guilt approach in a way that only grandmothers can. She tried to explain to me that I was letting my teammates down and that I was leaving them out there to handle the second half one woman down. They needed me blah blah blah. I gave a slight edgeways glance to the huddle and saw my sister looking at me pleadingly. I was conflicted, but my prideful stubbornness had fully kicked in at this point. No way was I going back out there to the 'unfairness' – or in hindsight, to lose.

The worst of it was that I hadn't really thought this through. You see, my sister was still playing, so I had to sit there in the car, watching my team get thrashed through the whole second half and waiting until the match was over so my sister could get a lift home. My earlier righteous independence was now starting to look a bit childish, and it was not lost on me. I started having mega second thoughts about this whole thing. I knew I had made a big mistake. I had let my team down, my coach down, my sister down, my grandmother down, but mostly I had let myself down. It wasn't just about the losing – even if I had gone back out there and played, we were never going to win, but that wasn't the point. Being honest with myself, I knew I had been intimidated and outplayed by this rough, but also genuinely skilled, opponent. I wasn't good enough for the challenge, and I didn't like it. I got scared. I was losing. I was embarrassed. I wilted. And I quit. No other way to say it. I. QUIT.

Even as a still maturing 11-year-old girl, I knew that I had done something wrong. And I had humiliated myself in the process. Even my little sister, who was trying her best but not having much success keeping the sliotar (the Irish word for the specific game ball) out of the back of the net, stuck it out. In her defence, she was only put in goal as she was the youngest on the pitch, and the coach wanted to protect her from the more developed 16-year-old players. In very immediate hindsight, quitting didn't sit well with me. In fact, it felt wrong down to my core. I'd always been the ambitious overachiever kid, and I wasn't proud of myself. Even saying it now stings a little. I quit, and I hated that I did it. So I decided, on that car ride home, that I was never going to do it again. I didn't want to be a quitter or, even worse, be known as a quitter, and so I have never let it happen again. I've come close, more times than I'd like to admit, but I have always managed to tough it out and not run away from any of the challenges since thrown my way.

MOTIVATION AND PURPOSE

I truly believe that the starting point of any success is motivation. We are each defined and driven by our own individual motivations. Motivation is personal: you can't be given it, someone can't define it for you, but it can and will define you. Quitting that day made me promise my 11-year-old self that I would never quit on opportunity again, and that has been my lifelong motivation.

So while that was among the least proud moments of my career in sports, I have been blessed to have had more prideful ones on my journey to date. I've always been a tad uncomfortable with showing and expressing pride in my own accomplishments; I think it's part and parcel of being Irish. Just recently, I won the Distinguished Alumni Award at Sacred Heart University. I was surprised when I learnt that my teammates had quietly recommended me for the 'Community Award' due to some of my volunteering work (more about that later). In doing so, they gathered a lot of supporting material from both my career and volunteering work to prepare the submission, and ultimately the awarding committee deemed my path as an exemplary one to serve as an example to current students of what can be achieved in your first 10–20 years upon graduation. Beyond surprise, I was also honoured and humbled by the recognition, and it reminded me that it is important to show humility and gratitude for the wins along the way. I hadn't sought reward for this work, and rather did it fairly quietly beyond raising awareness for some of the strategic initiatives, be it for work or for fundraising. And while there is honour in keeping your head down and doing the quiet work, there is also a need to champion the efforts of the collective. Some of the projects are long, and celebrating small wins motivates and engages people. It serves as a short term energy boost that fuels the longer-term successful outcome. It can seem trivial and frivolous at the time, but I've learnt that without it, some of the people and some of the projects will not make it to the finish line. It took me a long time to learn this, and I have to actively remind myself to pause and reflect on the progress, and acknowledge that with my peers. In my acceptance speech, I spoke about my self-doubt when arriving at SHU, the challenges of being a student-athlete, but came back to my promise of not wasting my opportunity.

I've been part of many great championship teams, and I've won medals, trophies and accolades throughout my sporting, academic and working career. I have been trusted to lead teams on and off the courts and fields of play. Collectively and individually, there have been countless struggles and successes that have all challenged me and my teams to go beyond our comfort zone. But when you go beyond that comfort zone, that's where the real impact is. My proudest moment is not the 25-million-dollar brand store that my team designed and executed on 5th Ave., New York. It is not the award-winning style store we created in Tokyo, Japan, and it is not winning any basketball titles, accolades, championships or MVP awards. It's both bigger and smaller than that. It is more meaningful and purposeful.

My proudest moment to date was back in July 2018. I walked down a severely pot-holed dirt road and entered through a 10 feet barbed wire security gate into the Republic of Congo's (DRC) first international school. I was struck with a simultaneous feeling of disbelief and pride. Right in front of me was the reality of an idea, a dream that I had first sketched on paper two years earlier. I was fortunate enough to have had the opportunity to travel to the Republic of Congo to teach basketball to young kids at a nonprofit organization and partner of adidas' adiFund (a volunteer programme for adidas employees). I played lunchtime basketball with some colleagues, and one of them suggested I go on this trip as there were a lot of girls in the programme and not many role models. (I was one of two women who played lunchtime basketball at adidas.) Hearing about the opportunity, I was immediately interested and just made the cut-off time to apply and get my travel visa approved. That trip to Goma was transformational for me in so many ways. I was able to spend time and connect with the founder of the organization, Dario. Dario is a realist and a dreamer all rolled into one. He grew up in Goma, lived through the Rwanda genocide and was spared his life in his teenage years by relocating to Belgium to complete high school. Dario, like me, has a love for basketball and played it every day in Belgium, continuing to play it daily when he returned to Goma as an empowered university graduate, ready to tackle his biggest project yet – rebuilding Goma. What started as a morning basketball run with his close friends turned into an improvised coaching clinic for young kids hanging out by the courts. More and more kids would show up, and a couple of years later Promo Jeune Basket (PJB) was formed. Today, it is an organization that supports over 1,000 kids in Goma, using basketball as the vehicle for youth development and education, with one of those kids now actually playing for the Golden State Warriors in the NBA. This is the power of Dario. During a car ride across Goma, Dario learnt that I was an architect and immediately saw me as a resource that he didn't have. When you have dreams like Dario's, you know you can't do it alone, and have to be able to beg, borrow and steal people's time and hearts to get anything done. He shared his dream for the future of Goma – PJB was just the start, but international standard education would be the critical unlock to larger scale infrastructure and economic development in the DRC.

While building an international school wasn't my personal dream, it quickly became my purpose, and I was blessed to have some ingredients that Dario did not have. I had the ability to articulate his vision through a compelling architectural design. I was able to translate his description of his dream into a tangible design scheme that could be first used to secure funding, and eventually serve as the architectural drawings to get the campus built. At the time I didn't appreciate how valuable this was and was legitimately just happy to help him out. In my spare time, I worked on all phases of the design development and even helped pitch the project to key investors on a repeat visit the following summer. The site had been cleared and construction was underway. It was truly amazing to see. So when I returned for a third time, in July 2018, and entered that gate, and saw our entire vision brought to life with the sounds of children laughing and playing, I was overwhelmed with emotion. This was a project that was actively changing people's lives and changing the future of a whole community.

It was truly a full-circle moment for me. Basketball unlocked my own college education. My education got me a career in the sports industry.

And through this, I was able to visit Goma and meet Dario. And Dario was able to challenge and inspire me to believe that his dream was possible. The irony here is that while I depended on Dario for that belief, he was depending on me to bring his vision to life. I had never seen it that way until walking through those gates and seeing the pride in his eyes. He walked me over to the heart of the campus, the first roofed basketball court in the DRC, and there beside the door was a placard with my name on it. The name of the same small kid who had wished her village had an indoor court when she first fell in love with the game. I could never have dreamt that I would design and build a basketball court, never mind travelling to Africa and designing an international school in DRC. And to top it off, that gym would have a dedication to me. I was both incredibly humbled and massively proud. I was shown once again that sport truly does have the power to change lives.

CHALLENGES

Throughout my career in sport, there have been many hurdles I've faced en route to success. I've heard people say no journey is easy just as no friendship is filled with only laughter. But it's overcoming the hard parts that makes the outcome even more fulfilling and rewarding. I have learnt to embrace the journey and see it as part of my mission to continuously learn and improve. I know that I will be better a year from now than I am today, but I can't get there if I don't take the next step and acknowledge that it is all a learning curve. It may not have always been clear to me, especially during the toughest moments or on the toughest days. I always wanted to be good, to be great even, but I just wasn't always sure that I could be. I was fortunate to have great school and club coaches along the way and to have family that supported me on my journey.

Being honest, I think some of the hurdles have been things that I've put in front of myself, essentially me getting in my own way. There have been times where I haven't been as confident in myself as I could've been. It was something of an invisible hurdle that I created for myself, not always obvious to other people. I was brought up to be humble, but when it came to competing, I wished at times that I was more confident in the moment. Sometimes I would try the whole 'fake it till you make it', and sometimes that worked. Other times it made me be perceived as cocky or nonchalant even; I can tell you honestly, that I was never either of these, not deep down, not in my mind and not in my character at all. I learnt this the hard way when playing on the national team. I had broken my wrist and missed taking part in full team practices. I was there, shooting around with my left hand, and doing my conditioning but couldn't compete. I finally came back from injury the weekend that we had two friendlies against England. Needless to say, I didn't get many playing minutes, and so I was very disappointed. After the second game, my coach approached me to talk to me. I thought he was going to console me, but instead he berated me for 'swanning around' and expecting that I had a birthright to my starting spot. I was shell-shocked because deep down I had felt super insecure about getting my place back in the lineup, and I thought I was trying to be positive, stay upbeat and cheer on my team. I might have overdone it. He thought I was taking things for granted and told me in not-so-kind words that I needed to get off my butt, work harder to make up for lost time and show him that I had earned those minutes back. While I hadn't been taking anything for granted, it didn't matter as he didn't see it that way. I had to double down and make sure he would never have a reason to say that to me again. In hindsight, I probably should've gone and asked him what he thought I needed to do to get back in the lineup, to show that I was ready to get back to work and understood that I would need to earn my spot again.

I'm the type of player and person who wants my work to speak for itself, and I trust that the tangibles and intangibles of that work will be seen by those who matter. For most of my sports career, I was an all-rounder, a person who would get the job done for the team, and was seen as the 'glue' of the team. I could pass, play defense, and wasn't afraid to put my body on the line; I was tough. Sometimes that showed in the stats, and sometimes it didn't. There was usually a higher-profile scorer, passer or defender, and often they got the recognition. I was usually okay with that because I knew I was solid, rarely outworked and valuable to the team. For the most part, I had coaches who recognized and celebrated that, and I developed a trusted rapport over time. When I've taken on new roles, I've been told that what I had done to get here wasn't going to be what got me to the next level. Or in another case, I was told I was hired for my expertise but that I would need to demonstrate it all over again in the job. It can be confusing and sometimes demotivating to be told those things, and seeking clarity is imperative. When faced with cross-functional work or a new team environment, I've learnt that it's always best to communicate expectations and spend the time to learn about each other's different strengths for a collectively stronger outcome. The sooner this is done, the sooner real progress towards shared goals can be made. I still need to remind myself to do this daily in my job, and I have learnt that it's not always easy to talk about our strengths and weaknesses. But by being open, and looking to bolster your weaknesses through others' strengths, we can learn and grow from each other and not try to hide those weaknesses out of insecurity. Eventually, our weakness too get stronger as we learn and develop from those around us.

Like my basketball playing days, I'm sure my career will continue to be faced with hurdles. I have confidence that the experience I have gained so far will become even more useful in helping me overcome future unforeseen hurdles. As I've grown and developed in my career, I've cemented more confidence in myself and in my approach. The key is not to lose who you are or compromise your character. You have to balance who you are at the core with who you evolve to become over time. You need to build relationships, advocate for others, genuinely find common ground and understand other people's motivations. To do that, you have to be authentic and put yourself out there, spend time with your colleagues, listen to them and learn about their challenges. You need to know how you can help them. By knowing this, you can be of value to them. This is commonly known as servant leadership, and this works in all directions in the organization. You need to know how you can help your peers, your boss and your team that reports to you.

I've learnt that great leadership is not about hierarchy, but it is about experience, and it takes time to learn and put into action. Over the years, I've experienced both bad managers and great leaders, and I've learnt to spot the difference. Bad managers can be dogmatic and bend you to their will, and you usually end up a little resentful. Great leaders help you understand how you can be at your best for the team, and you become flexible to deliver what the team needs. You understand your role and willingly do it to the best of your ability. This has been true in both my playing days and in my career.

BALANCE

As I strive to be a great leader, I have noticed that the value my team bring to the organization hasn't always been recognized for a variety of reasons. Workplace competition can be different from team sports. For starters, the playing field has been more dominated by men. While we are technically all working for the same company, we aren't necessarily on the same team. Culturally, the value systems have varied, and in most cases, self-advocacy is a critical component of career progression in the organizational hierarchy. You cannot solely rely on rapport between you and your boss or a peer. The corporate world has a different set of rules, and there is always a game to be played. Navigating that dynamic environment can be challenging and exhausting, all while doing your actual job.

As recently as this past year, I've had challenging moments that have made me question myself, my skills and really shaken my confidence at times. In the moment, I allowed it to consume me too much, which distracted me from performing well. This hindrance to performance further shook my confidence and made me nervous that my reputation would come into question. It took time for me to recentre, focus on what I could control and concentrate on the work at hand. In the end, reason and my preparedness prevailed, and I came out the other side successful, albeit a little bruised and battered.

That cycle of stress and worry is not sustainable, and luckily the Christmas holidays created a natural break, allowing me time with family and time to rest, reflect and reset. No matter how much experience we have, we aren't bulletproof, and we all need an off-season to balance the demands of the season. There will always be tough projects and tough personalities to work with, and navigating those situations can be stressful. I've learnt that staying balanced is key.

While I'm not playing much basketball or team sports these days, I have found other ways to maintain balance. I love to try new things, and currently occupy my free time trying new sports and particularly love playing tennis, winter skiing, hiking, surfing and even kitesurfing (this one is a little extreme). For me, I find that challenging my body, learning new movements and wiring new connections in my brain is a balancing of the scales. Being able to take my mind off of work gives me more inspiration and energy to actually tackle it head-on. I know that I need daily, weekly, monthly and seasonal breaks to be able to perform at my best. Even the top athletes know they need to take frequent breaks in play in order to recover and go again. Covid-19 has caused companies to wake up to this idea too, and we see more and more offering additional health and wellness benefits in response to employee requests. Nike instituted a company-wide wellness week in August 2020, allowing employees an additional week to rest, spend time with family or pursue their passions outside of work. There is more and more evidence to support less workplace illness, more motivated and engaged employees, as well as zero reduction in overall annual employee productivity.

WORK IS PLAY. PLAY IS WORK.

My professional corporate career has been much like my basketball career: a cycle of seasons, so to speak. A career is not static and requires taking on new challenges and working with new teams. With each new job or promotion, you need to recognize that in some capacity, you are going to be a rookie in the role, and you may find yourself being unsure of exactly how you are going to succeed. But by being willing to learn from others and investing time in yourself to grow your skills, you are preparing yourself for when the time comes to put those skills to the test and overcome new challenging situations. Each time we succeed, growth and confidence come, and before you know it, the new season is complete. Having that sophomore mentality and digging deep, persevering and earning the right to be seen and trusted as a solid team player in your role comes next. You evolve with experience and become a seasoned veteran, leading by example. You find yourself captaining the ship, inspiring the team and ultimately bringing out the best in others. It truly is a cycle of growth, where I have continued to experience the nervousness, the self-doubt, the learning and the leading. Once the challenge has been overcome, and I have delivered success, I get hungry for the next challenge, and the curiosity for the unknown takes over again. My batteries are recharged by the next new challenge, new environment, new team and new players, and the cycle starts over again.

I don't know what is next for me, but I do know that I am currently in a role where I have just experienced some serious growth in the sophomore phase of the cycle. During the pandemic, I moved to Oregon to take on my dream role at Nike, a new company for me. I was recruited for the role, and on paper it had all the ingredients of my dream job. Onboarding during the pandemic was rough, and trying to learn the culture of the company was hard to do remotely from the spare bedroom in my house. It was hard to make a genuine personal connection with some people. There were some team issues that really challenged me, both intellectually and emotionally. Some really humbled me, and ultimately, I learnt a lot. I once read, 'The degree to which a person can grow is directly proportional to the amount of truth they can accept about themselves without running away.' There were times in my rookie year when I truly felt like the 11-year-old me, facing an arduous challenge and feeling like I was losing. Admittedly, the temptation to quit was there. And yet again, this time it could've been easy to take the easy way out; people would've understood, it was a tough time compounded by the pandemic, lockdowns and social unrest that had overtaken much of the USA during the same year. But I weathered it, pushed through, and yet again learnt a lot about myself. I persevered and overcame some big hurdles. When it was really hard, I sought advice from other fearless leaders that I admired in the company, and unsurprisingly, I learnt that they all had their tough moments, tough days and even tough weeks too. It is all part of it, and it is something that I now remind my mentees of too. I have been rebuilding and leading a re-energized team tasked with a very exciting project for the top sports brand in the world. We really hit our stride as a team, and I know wholeheartedly that I want to and will see it through. We will deliver on our goals, we will have our championship moment and we will celebrate as a team. And then, after all of that, who knows, maybe I will be ready to start eyeing my next challenge.

MY RECIPE

Hard work, grit and embracing an attitude of 'why not me?'

Looking back on my journey, I realize that the most significant obstacle I had to overcome was my own self-doubt. I wish I could go back in time and tell my younger self to be more confident, more courageous and to embrace the attitude of 'why not me?'

Believing in yourself is the first step towards reaching your dreams, but it's the grit and hustle that breathe life into that belief. It's easy to look at others' success and assume they have some innate talent or unique advantage, but in reality, most of the successful people we admire got there through hard work, dedication and a willingness to take risks.

We are the creators of our own futures, but it takes more than just hard work to achieve our dreams. We also need mentors, supporters and a little bit of luck along the way. We need to be open to change, willing to see opportunities when they arise and brave enough to seize them.

So, to anyone who may be struggling with self-doubt or feeling intimidated by the success of others, I say this: don't be afraid to ask yourself, 'why not me?' Believe in yourself, commit to the hard work and never give up on your dreams. The 'why not me?' mentality has the potential to take you on an incredible journey.

CHAPTER 3
Callary on Coaching

Dr. Bettina Callary

'Callary on Coaching'. That's the title of my best-selling book, according to the dream my dad told me he had. He told me I needed to write a book and it would be a best-seller. Well, that is audacious. I'll start with a chapter. I have some great supporters. My family, my partner, Tom, who tells my three kids (and they believe) that their mom is capable of anything and everything. So, who am I? I am Dr. Bettina Callary, Canada Research Chair in sport coaching and adult learning, Associate Professor, Editor-in-Chief of the *International Sport Coaching Journal* (ISCJ), supervisor, coach, coach developer, athlete, partner, mother, daughter, sibling, friend. I am 40 years old and have been a researcher for 18 years and a coach for 25. Along the way, I coached for local ski clubs, elite youth teams, provincial teams, the Argentina World Cup ski team, the Canadian Alpine Ski Team and most recently coaching my own children. I love coaching. I also love research and the opportunity to supervise and mentor students in research. I think I have always made good use of my time and seized opportunities as they arose (of which I have been privileged to have many), which is perhaps why I am where I am now.

In November 2021, I was the keynote speaker at the Global Coach Conference for the International Council of Coaching Excellence (ICCE) in Portugal. I spoke about what I see as the state of coaching research: Sport coaching research is a young field that has its roots derived largely from sport psychology researchers, many key white male figures over the past 40 years. I referred to them as our 'fathers' of the field. But as coaching research has progressively developed as a field of its own, we cannot forget its 'mothers' that have made impacts around the world and continue to drive the research forward. Being aware of the number of important women in our field, since I became the editor of ISCJ in 2020, I have added 12 new editorial board members, focusing on bringing more women to leadership. In 2022, the editorial board comprised of 57% female academics in our field. In Human Kinetics journals, 11 out of 27 editors are women, but I am not sure of the percentage of women board members. I feel this is an important mission because diversity in committees and boards ensures that a range of perspectives are honoured.

PERSPECTIVE

My entry into the scholarship of coaching started in practice. I started coaching while in high school because it got me a free ski pass and it was fun to work with kids. I was too young to get the coaching certification but volunteered with the five-year-old pre-race group. I was also on my race team at school. I was a little envious that I was not as good as others because they were on club teams outside of school, but in hindsight, I was actually as fast if not faster than many of them and I had their respect. The next December, I took my level one coaching course. I was sure my friends would get certified and I would fail. In fact, I was the only one to pass. I remember that the evaluators told me that I could adapt as they requested. And so, I coached a group of seven-year-olds. We played games, skied a lot and improved. I moved up through the ski school race programme and after high school, spent a winter in the Rocky Mountains as a full-time ski instructor. There, I met my future husband, Tom – a snowboarder! I soon taught him to ski and then to coach.

By my first year of university, I was coaching the club team. My fellow coaches became my good friends as I spent considerable time coaching. At this time, I also trained for my next certification level. To pass the courses, the coach had to demonstrate both the ability to pedagogically coach well and to ski above the level of the athletes they coached (to demonstrate effectively). Because I had not raced at a club level, I began an arduous training regimen to get myself to the level I needed. Setting gates (training courses) is a physical endeavour – I needed to organize and carry a bundle of (heavy) gates on my shoulders while on skis, drill a hole into the snow (while propping gates on my hip) and (at that time) screw the gates into the hole. I then visualized the course I wanted to set, measured the distance to where the next gate would be set and repeated this process many times. In my dogged dedication, I became coordinated and strong, setting gates often solo, to then train in the courses that I set.

Pedagogically, I took courses in Human Kinetics for my Bachelor of Science and applied what I learned on the ski hills. By my fourth year, I had attained my level three ski instructor (out of four levels) and was prepared to take the level three ski coaching exam (the last ski level), which, the evaluator decided, would involve skiing in the same course as the women from the Canadian national team, who happened to be training there. I was terrified, skied my heart out, laughed and cried, and importantly, I passed! At that time, I was one of the few women to have attained that level of coaching in Canada. One of the other women, Marie-Pierre Jourdain, is someone that I have maintained a special bond with some 20 years later. While I didn't know all the women at that level, and we were relatively isolated, we also had a respect and understanding that came with the territory that we could feel confident about. I was immediately recruited to be a coach developer for a level one coaching course and proceeded to give courses to coaches for the next seven years on a regular basis.

Coaching at our club in my final year of my bachelor's degree, we had the privilege of having a family visiting from Argentina coach with us. The Simaris' three adult children raced on the World Cup circuit, and ordinarily the parents were their coaches. The youngest, still a child, was enrolled in our club. Teresita and Mario Simari inspired me to want to coach at the highest levels. Teresita was the first woman that I had ever met who had coached World Cup. She was a fantastic mentor, inspiring me with her lived experiences. She had made a career out of coaching and had developed and fostered athletes' progress to the highest levels in their sport. She was a quiet do-er, and she got the job done. I appreciated this about her, and she was unassuming in showing me how she had accomplished her dream. Prior to the 2006 Torino Winter Olympics, I was invited to work with the Simaris in Argentina as a coach with their World Cup and development teams during the Northern summer of 2005, with expenses paid, albeit not otherwise paid. I jumped at the opportunity. Tom was invited to coach as well, as the extra set of hands were welcome. In Argentina, our team trained with many World Cup teams as we traveled the South American Cup circuit. The training was intense, the volume of travel was immense, driving to all the mountains in Argentina and Chile, living in cramped quarters, cooking, cleaning, organizing dryland and on-snow training, setting courses, attending races, often in high altitude. There was no time for rest, no time to get sick, no time to recuperate. The Simaris appeared to be used to this chaotic schedule. I found it exhausting. At the end of the season, I was invited to continue to coach the team, following them to Europe and towards the Olympic Games, with only expenses taken care of, as before. But only I could go, not Tom. At the same time, I had received a full scholarship for a master's in sport psychology at the University of Ottawa. I was burnt out. I was not willing to give up on my life with Tom (we were engaged at that time), and I went back to Canada.

While I pursued my master's, I coached the club team with a new focus. I felt confident inspiring athletes and their parents on a high performance trajectory, and they did well! I was the head coach of my age group team, with 4 coaches who worked for me (including Tom) and 60 athletes1. That year, I was provincial Coach of the Year for development level athletes (across all sports). Several athletes joined the elite regional team (one making it as far as the Canadian national development team

---

[1] As an aside, Tom and I were married that summer and our athletes surprised us by showing up after our ceremony with an arc of ski poles that we were ushered through. A short note from Tom is included at the end of this chapter.

in time). The following year, I pursued my diploma in high performance coaching through the Coaching Association of Canada (CAC). I relished in learning about coaching and taking the modules that allowed me to understand all that I was putting into practice. I was passionate about my master's degree research: preparing for and doing an intervention aimed at helping a volleyball coach learn how he could help his team self-regulate, leading to a championship. I was then invited to volunteer guest coach with the Canadian Alpine Ski Team's women's speed team. This two-week camp was an amazing occasion to see how the Canadian team operated and learn from excellent national team coaches. Soon thereafter, the women's technical head coach, Tim Gfeller, invited me to volunteer another coach camp. I was then invited to yet another camp. I loved these opportunities, appreciating working with professional, hard-working, knowledgeable coaches and athletes. I also noticed quickly that I was the only woman coach there and had many conversations questioning where were the women. It must be noted that due to the brevity of this chapter, I have excluded the hardships, sexist comments and microaggressions from male coaches who I've decided do not get the honour of being included in this chapter, as their actions do not warrant inclusion in a chapter about success. However, of course, these individuals exist and are a constant drain on mental and emotional energy. Indeed, in hindsight, I now realize that I was working with some athletes who had been under tremendous stress and abused by a former male coach who was later convicted of sexual abuse, and it was probably crucial that I was at these camps to provide a better balance to the coaching staff, made up of all men. At the time, I did not know the history and I was sheltered from the stories; nonetheless, many staff asked me when I would sign a full-time contract and I told them I too was awaiting that dream. And so I dreamed. I wrote a 10-year plan in which I was coaching the national team, but in those dreams I also had my husband and our (yet-to-be-conceived) child who came along to training camps and races. As I was finishing my master's, and the academic side pushed me to do what everyone was doing, I applied for scholarships towards my PhD.

It was then, at one of the national team camps, that I talked to a strength and conditioning coach one evening around the dinner table. Why did he keep seeing me at these camps? Well, I kept getting invited back. I hoped it might turn into something more permanent (and paid). His reply: 'Bettina, a woman coaching at this level? It's like me saying I want to be a super-model. It's just never going to happen'. I was floored. I had been moving along so nicely. Everything seemed to be falling in place. But, again in hindsight, while poorly expressed, he had a point. No women were hired as coaches on the national team. My contract never came. In fact, at the time of writing this chapter, for the 2022–2023 season, Alpine Canada hired its first ever female head coach. In 2008, mine was a pipedream.

That next week, I received a full scholarship to start my PhD in understanding the lifelong learning experiences of women coaches. My supervisors were Dr. Penny Werthner, who I believe to be one of the best practical academics in sport psychology and women in coaching, and Dr. Pierre Trudel, one of coaching research's 'fathers'. Thus started my next stage of academics, wherein I dove into the research on coaching. I was also coaching the elite regional team, but I was burning out again. I was passionate but was not safeguarding my mental and physical health, and as a result I got very sick, continuing to try to coach through it, and feeling totally crummy. I also got paid very little, a $10,000 stipend for the year. Nonetheless, I doggedly pursued coaching opportunities, when I was offered head coach of the Canadian university men's alpine ski team at the World University Games in 2008. The manager of the team, Richard LePage, got a grant through 'women in coaching', to support the expenses for me and my friend Marie-Pierre as the two coaches. Two women! That was a first. We were the only team to have two women coaches at the Games.

In case my life was not busy enough, I decided to have a baby. Anneka arrived in the summer of 2009. Coaching took a back seat as I navigated motherhood. There was no opportunity to coach with a baby on board. I helped out with the club team. I facilitated a couple of coaching courses. I focused on my PhD. By the third year of my PhD, I had realized that perhaps academia was an interesting path. I could 'coach' students, continue to learn about what I was passionate, and not burn myself out or leave my family for long periods. While I continued to coach throughout my PhD, because it was so drastically different than it had been in the years before becoming a mother, I felt my identity had changed and I felt like an imposter when I talked about being a coach because I was no longer on the high performance pathway. I had a second child, Julia, at the tail end of my PhD. I applied for a few positions, accepting one at Cape Breton University (CBU), mere weeks after defending my PhD. We moved to Nova Scotia, and I had a son, Alex, a few years after that.

Fast forward to present day – I have been a professor for 10 years. Coaching is such a fascinating topic to research because of its incredible vastness. I am a coach if I coach one hour per week for my children's basketball school team. I am a coach if I take Swimming 101 and volunteer coach two or three times per week for my daughters' swim team. I am a coach if I coach the recreationally competitive master skiers at the local hill. I am a coach when I coached the Nova Scotia ski team at the Canada Games. I am a coach developer if I facilitate ski courses, or if I teach university courses in coaching to students who are coaches. I used to feel like I was only a coach if it was my career, as a professional full-time paid Olympic coach. But now I know that I am a coach if I'm a mother, a woman, a professor, if I have little training or lots. And coaching is so much more than technical skill development. Researching and practising the craft of coaching keeps me forever learning and curious. I can continue to research marginalized and equity-deserving groups in sport and coaching and the questions will never dry up.

ACADEMIC FOCUS

I dove into the academics of coaching much in the same way as I did my coaching practice, learning as much as possible. In academia, I haven't had the blatant 'glass ceiling' with no contract. I have been able to forge a path to excellence, pursue committee work that I have wanted to be involved in (much of it volunteer), take on the opportunities presented, apply for grants and the Canada Research Chair (CRC) position. I was offered the opportunity to take on the role of editor for the ISCJ, which came with immense responsibility with regard to making decisions about a lot of the coaching research that gets published as well as taking leadership in the ICCE's Research Committee and planning and adjudicating the presentations for the Global Coach Conference. Academia is also competitive in terms of pushing oneself to achieve. There is a danger of getting caught in the rat race of academic 'publish or perish'. Women in academia are not immune to the social pressure of women in society in general. Especially in our field, we are still outnumbered by men.

I was recently asked to be a panel discussant at the launch of the framework and self-assessment for organizations regarding Gender Equity in Coaching through Canadian Women and Sport. This is a project that I was proud to play a small part in, as it serves as a workshop and web-based tool for organizations to use to create action plans for being more inclusive of women in coaching. I (very) briefly told my story to the 200+ participants who were tuned in for the webinar. At the end of my synopsis, Isabelle Cayer, the 'women in coaching' consultant for the CAC, laughed as she said that she's heard my story before and pointed out that I was left out of high performance coaching and so I went on to become one of the leading expert academics on the topic. The irony is clear. There's still so much work to do. In the academic world, we are plagued with gender imbalances and disparities, and yet it's so much better than in sport. What mountains we must climb! Luckily, from what I see in our field of sport coaching researchers, there are determined and outstanding women who can climb mountains, ski down them, and who appear to be willing to lend a hand when we fall or set up a chair when we need a rest.

CBU is a small undergraduate, teaching-focused university on an isolated island about as far East as you can go in Canada. I chose CBU because the pedagogical style resonated with coaching. I could teach community-based, experiential, small-group and interdisciplinary projects. Further, I was tasked with developing the suite of sport courses into a major. Thus, I developed a social science-based sport degree. The Sport and Physical Activity Leadership programme includes four streams of courses: coaching, outdoor leadership, sport management, and health and wellness. The small class sizes allow for fun and engaging teaching approaches, assignments and evaluations, wherein I often work with community partners in sport and recreation across this island that is a mecca for outdoor physical activity pursuits. During my interview for this position in 2012, one of my (now) colleagues, Dr. Jane Connell, mentioned that there was a large percentage of ageing adults on the island, and had I ever considered looking into research with aging adults in sport? When I accepted the position, my first research endeavour was to partner with a colleague from the University of Ottawa, Dr. Bradley Young, whom I knew to be a leading expert on the psychology of Masters Athletes, and asked him if he wanted to apply for a grant with me on coaching Masters Athletes. This began a muti-year research programme that is still ongoing and growing in 2022. Our lead PhD student research assistant, Scott Rathwell, who studied emerging adults in sport for his dissertation, got a job at the University of Lethbridge as a professor with expertise in ageing adults in sport as a direct result of his contribution to our research programme. With two federally funded Social Sciences and Humanities Research Council (SSHRC) grants to support our research, the three of us now collaborate as the pan-Canadian research group: Coaching Masters Athletes (coachingmastersathletes.com). In 2021, we wrote a book published by Routledge, which the publishing company commissioned because of growing interest in the topic.

My original research interests in the professional development of coaches' psychosocial approaches (from my master's), and my interest in lifelong learning and 'women in sport' coaching (from my PhD) have, of course, persisted. Thus, my research programme forks various coach and coach development research with, about and for equity-deserving and marginalized populations and contexts. Having a strong foundation in sport psychology, I have also moved towards sport sociology, with increasing attention focused on sociocultural issues of gender, race, culture and age, to more fully encapsulate psychosocial approaches to inclusive coaching.

My research came to a head in 2018 as I applied for, was selected and then together with my institution applied for the tier 2 (emerging researcher) CRC in Sport Coaching and Adult Learning (a title which I developed and was approved by my institution around themes of health and wellbeing). While on sabbatical in 2018 at the University of Queensland, Australia, and picking up different ideas and perspectives of sport from around the world, I also composed a foundational book for coach developers on instructional strategies for coach education, published by Routledge and co-edited with Dr. Brian Gearity from the University of Denver. At this time, I was accepted into the Nippon Sport Science University's Coach Developer Academy, which involved an exclusive and highly competitive application process into the fifth cohort (out of seven total), composed of 12 individuals (coaching researchers, national multi-sport coach developers and national sport specific coach developers). In this capacity, I became part of a tight network of coach developers and coaching researchers from across the world, and I had the opportunity to work with coaches from developing nations who aspired to coach at the Tokyo Paralympics.

In 2019, I became the CRC, where 90% of my job was research oriented. I also received funding from the Canada Foundation for Innovation to set up the CoASTaL lab (Community Active Sport Training and Learning Lab). Thus, I proceeded to further develop my research in line with my CRC goals and set up my lab to foster research collaborations and excellence within and across the programme that I had created (and for which we hired two colleagues). I also applied for and received SSHRC grants for two new projects: one in understanding how strength and conditioning organizations and coach developers could foster psychological and sociocultural knowledge into their coach education, because I believe strongly in promoting coaching approaches that develop whole, psychologically healthy and sociologically safeguarded athletes. The second grant explores Mi'kmaq (Indigenous Peoples of Eastern Canada) ways of knowing about place-based cultural and spiritual sport participation, from the perspectives of coaches and youth involved in the Unama'ki surf programme.

In 2020, I was looking down the pipeline of about a dozen keynote invited presentations, with international travel at minimum twice per month in addition to being the principal investigator on three large federally funded projects. Then Covid-19 restrictions and lockdowns hit, and the trajectory of research pivoted mostly online. In hindsight, I was on a burnout path again, and I don't know how long I could have sustained that lifestyle, and the pandemic gave me a chance to prioritize my research and work. This is easier said than done, as tough decisions need to be made: I have always tried to take advantage of every opportunity, but found myself unable to do so moving forward. Honestly, what has given me the strength is the support I have from my family and colleagues, my passion for my work, my love of learning, my determination to live every day to its fullest and my ability, maybe subconscious, of finding a window when a door closes.

CONCLUSION

I close this chapter with a few lessons I have learned and thoughts about what the future holds. I don't make the rest of my life wait on career aspirations. I left coaching to stay with my life partner. I had two children during my PhD. I will not wait until I'm older, until I'm wiser, until I have more time, because I don't know if that time will ever happen. Instead, I take opportunities to see where they will lead. I also find and strive for quality in all that I do, including rest and relaxation. My university is small, and I suffered from an inferiority complex when I first started my job in academia because I was in a small, predominantly undergraduate, teaching-intensive university. However, just like feeling insecure in my first coaching certification courses in skiing, I found that I had respect and that I was adaptable. I've found that this environment allows me to have my research passion and drive, but does not have extrinsic motivators that would likely frustrate me. I can, if I want, take a step back when I need to rest. The pressures are not external, only internal. For me, that is key.

I would be remiss if I did not give credit to Tom for always being my support, fan, confidante and for being there to push me to take opportunities. His belief in me has spurred me to these challenges. His zest for life has inspired me to jump in with both feet. His own life choices have been carefully positioned to provide me the capability to have these experiences, and lead this fulfilling life.1 Likewise, at a young age, my parents were also so supportive (and continue to be from afar).

I mentioned that I once wrote a 10-year coaching plan. I was working on my High Performance Coaching Diploma. To get into the headspace for such a goal-setting activity, I imagined being in a cabin in the woods at the base of a mountain, getting ready to coach the national team, but with my husband and child with me. At that time, that part of my plan was an imaginary dream. But then, eight years later, I was coaching the Nova Scotia team for Canada Games, and doing a dryland training camp, staying in a cabin at the base of the ski hill, and I had brought my family (Tom and two children) with me (I was pregnant with our third). As I was walking down to breakfast, it hit me. My dream had become a reality, and it was so different than my 10-year coaching plan! I was not with the national team. I had let go of that goal. I was living on an island in Nova Scotia (which I never would have dreamed of) and working as a professor. But here I was in a different capacity, living out the dream.

Living with the understanding that opportunities present themselves and I take them, the possibilities of long-term goals are endless. I am a lifelong learner and appreciate choice. I am inspired by learning and look

---

[1]This note is written from Tom: Bettina is a natural leader and excels in all that she puts her mind to. We are a team. With regard to our lives together, I'll use the sport analogy from cycling. In a cycling team, one athlete is protected, she is the GC leader. The others are 'domestiques'. The team works together to get the team jersey onto the podium (in our case, to have the best version of our joint life), and that means accepting the work that's being done for you, but also making that work easier by setting yourself up well and taking opportunities. That's how we operate, and it brings us happiness, success and a fun adventure-filled life.

for opportunities to inspire others in the scholarship of coaching. Thinking through how I have navigated the male-dominated world of sport coaching (both in practice and in research), I have carved out my own space while working within the current space. Why do I study equity-deserving and marginalized groups? I was provoked to study women in coaching from my own ski coaching experiences. I was impelled to study the psychosocial adult-oriented coaching approaches of working with ageing adults because of my move to Cape Breton Island, which similarly has encouraged me to enter into the process of reconciliation in my job and in my life in doing participatory action research with the Indigenous communities on the island. Living in Cape Breton with so many Indigenous peoples, and with the privilege and responsibility of being a CRC in sport coaching and adult learning, I am intrinsically motivated to not just acknowledge where I live and come from, but to support, provide service and make a difference to my community. My experiences with coaches who simply do not consider the psychosocial and sociocultural side of the relationships that they are in have prompted my interest in coaches developing whole athletes. My children's sport experiences and coaching them have also generated interest in understanding philosophies of youth sport that extend beyond coach/athlete-centredness and towards place-based community participation, ability/disability and hidden disability. My personal experiences and observations of the world around me abound with the reasons why I study what I do. From my high performance ski coaching days, I have a dogged determination and perseverance in my passion for sport, but there is a lot wrong with it. From my days in high-performance ski coaching, I developed a relentless determination and deep passion for sport. Yet, I recognize its flaws. Still, there are moments of brilliance, and pockets of excellence that I actively seek out, learn from, and find great joy in. I seek out those fantastic pockets and learn from them, and this brings me much joy. I know that whatever comes, this is what's next for Bettina Callary. Would I do anything differently? Probably not. I have learned over time to have a completely different view of coaching than I used to, and I like the expansiveness of what I see.

CHAPTER **4**

'Indian disability sport'
Thriving through adversity
Dr. Padmini Chennapragada

'When anyone tells me I can't do anything ... I'm just not listening anymore.'

Florence Griffith Joyner

In 2010, I was searching the internet for a quote that I could add to the acknowledgements page of my final year undergraduate project report. Back then, while the quote got my attention, I did not realize how profoundly Florence Griffith Joyner's story would impact my life. I was reading her story at a time in my life when I was being told not to think beyond the box that was my education curriculum to become a physical therapist. I was studying in a physical therapy school that did not allow us to participate in using critical thinking or reasoning skills. Reading Joyner's story at once felt like talking to an old friend.

For as long as I can remember, I wasn't just that child who coloured outside the lines. I was a child who would want to sketch in a colouring class if that was what appealed to my senses. Coming from an orthodox South Indian Hindu family, compared to my peers at every level, I have lived a privileged life. I went to study at an English convent run by a Spain-based missionary group. My banker father saw the importance of learning the English language at an early age in his life. He wanted all his three children to be proficient in English because he felt it would open more opportunities for us. I was raised by parents who agreed with my approach of not colouring in a colouring class if my heart felt like sketching with just one colour. With such an upbringing, I ended up being the only member of my entire family on both sides who did not become an engineer or a doctor.

> *Having started my career as a physiotherapist in India, I was never satisfied with the answers I was finding to the questions that bothered me.*
> Why were mothers carrying their disabled children in their arms when wheelchairs lay around the hospital wards?
> Why don't we see more disabled people come to the physiotherapy clinic for therapies?

The questions were endless. I never stopped asking these questions and, in the early 2010s, my search led me to the United States. In 2021, I became the first Indian to ever graduate with a PhD in adapted physical education from the United States. In the last ten years, I have expanded the scope of my work to become a disability sport education consultant for many non-profits in India that serve children with disabilities. Within India, there is very little research and development work being conducted in the area of disability sport. Since 2015, I have promoted initiatives and activities in India that increase public discourse about sports for persons with disabilities. I investigate sport governance irregularities using India's information-seeking tool, the Right to Information Act (2005). Without seeking information that is deliberately not made available publicly, citizens with disabilities in India have long suffered many injustices. Through my work, I promote the advancement of democratic values inside the Indian sports ecosystem, which is largely dominated by leadership that is more politically motivated than one guided by science and scientists.

When I began my work in India, I was not well understood for several reasons. I found that there are many myths that surround conducting research efforts inside Indian disability sports. Resistance to any accountability measures introduced into the sector is high. Outside the power lobbies, entry for outsiders into the disability sport community is highly controlled. Some of the things that have been said to my face are:

'You will sell the data to foreigners and universities to earn money!'

'You do not have a disability, why do you work in this sector? There is no money in this!'

'You don't have a disability; you cannot work in this field!'

'You spent so much money and got educated in the United States. Why do you want to come and work in this corrupt mess?'

Beyond my role as a scholar-activist, I often interact with families of athletes with disabilities who are illiterate and need assistance to seek legal counsel for matters related to their child's sporting rights. A standard day in this part of my journey consists of educating the athletes or their support systems about the intricacies of the justice system. The proudest moment in my decade-long career working for persons with disabilities was when Mrs. Salamat, Sameeha Barvin's mother, called me to share the news of her daughter being included in the national list to represent India at the World Deaf Championships in Lublin, Poland. Sameeha Barvin was a Deaf athlete who was discriminated against from inclusion on an Indian national team because the national sport federation was not prepared to send female staff to Poland. The easiest solution to address their budgetary struggles was to prevent the inclusion of any women athletes even if they qualified. This news shook India's disability rights community intensely. The uproar resulted in creating huge support for her, as the Paralympic movement was receiving major cheering from the government and media alike. Being an invisible disability, Sameeha's status as a Deaf athlete was brushed aside. I volunteered my time as a subject matter expert for her case against the federation, which resulted in a landmark judgement from the Madras High Court in India.

I never met Sameeha until almost a year later when we travelled to a common city where we sat down to talk to one another through her mother. Sameeha's story, like that of many other Deaf athletes in India, is similar in educational struggles and lack of accessible formats of communication to socialize and experience true inclusion.

In the ten years that I have been working with people with disabilities, I have worked in different capacities to advance disability rights at the grassroots level in India. Sometimes, I am advocating for a child with their parents. On another day, I am accompanying an athlete to a lawyer's office or a sponsor who can fund their travel. While my roles shifted shades based on what was most needed at the time, I particularly excelled in roles where I had to do documentary research and establish a logical framework to seek legal relief on sport-related matters. Beyond these factors, in addition to being a woman, Sameeha's situation in India was exacerbated by the fact that her mother was a rights-based parent. Despite being denied the right to education for herself, Salamath fiercely championed her daughter. Coming from the southernmost tip of India, Sameeha and her mother went through extreme hardship advocating for her right to represent India as the only female Deaf athlete who qualified for the World Championships. On that fine evening when she left India to represent the country in Poland, Sameeha was the first female citizen of her village to go abroad and represent India at an international sporting event. When Sameeha competed on that rainy morning in Lublin, her YouTube live broadcast of the event was projected on a large screen in her village. Since her return from Poland, more children in her village go to the government playground to try and learn track and field activities. The village doesn't have dedicated sport coaching facilities or specific infrastructure. But as Sameeha dreams of cracking India's Civil Service Exams to become a government official, I am sure she will one day change how her village accesses sports for its children. I never had a plan to advocate or fight for someone like Sameeha. I woke up on a sleepy morning to a call from a fellow disability rights activist who insisted that I speak to Sameeha's mother. One initial phone call and I was in.

My own journey to survive an education system in India that did not allow free thinking and critical reasoning heavily influenced my everyday professional choice to be a scholar-activist. Having survived a system that ensures that it eliminates differently thinking individuals, I feel a natural draw to work on cases that require policy-level reforms as the only possible solution. While policy-level reforms are the hardest ones to achieve, I often see value in pushing for nothing less. This is because, beyond every Sameeha that comes to our attention for advocacy, there are a thousand others who can't even report the injustices they face inside Indian disability sport today.

In a sport ecosystem where most of the leadership is male and there is little room for growth for a woman of my standing, every day I learn a lesson on self-advocacy. In turn, I take these lessons and apply them to support athletes with disabilities who must fight many injustices inside the country to represent India at the international level.

RESISTANCE TO REPRESENTATION

When writing this chapter, It is now 2022, and it is still hard for me to get a spot at the table. Committees and commissions are announced by the Indian government to improve the state of sports in India. Rarely will these high-level committees include young professionals like me, whose work is focused on the intersectional space of disability rights and sporting rights. And now, when gender identity is applied to these contexts, the distance between us and these high-power spaces further increases. In case of invitations to speak on matters related to disability rights, I am often advised not to be fully honest with my input. I receive informal suggestions not to critique the ruling government in any shape or form. As extreme as it may seem, for a long time, as a scholar-activist, I have functioned on the border of not honouring the informal gag rule that exists inside Indian sports and staying away from critical commentary to appease the leadership to further gain access.

RESISTANCE TO RECOGNIZE

For years now, I have been Indian media's only subject matter source on all matters related to disability sport. Every time there was a major story or incident within the disability sport community, I was flooded with requests for information from media personnel (often men) who sought information from me, requested quick coaching on the matter and then went on to write the story as their own discovery. This happens to Indian women subject matter experts more often than one can imagine. As it continued to happen repeatedly, I learnt to identify people who would be my true allies versus those who would not authentically recognize my contribution to the sporting movement in India.

Interestingly, in March 2021, while reporting on a rights violation news article related to the Indian Paralympics, one sports journalist, *Sushmitha Ramakrishnan* (I can never forget her name), mentioned me as a researcher working on the politics of sports for the disabled in India. This development significantly impacted how I was approached by other journalists. Until then, it was taken for granted that I couldn't demand the right to be recognized for the research and advocacy work I was doing to promote disability sporting rights in India. When I look back, I feel Sushmitha turned the game for me with the way she wrote about me. Inside Indian sports journalism spaces, there are very few professionals like her. Many do not work in roles that have editorial freedom to report while considering variables like equity and gender parity.

Resistance to allowing women's entry into sport leadership spaces in India is quite well evident. The struggle is real, and it is a constant reminder for us to not slack in our work. Scaling back on our work to allow space for self-care and self-preservation is not option for women in Indian sports. Scaling back on work instantly is translated as hanging up our boots or falling out of the race. This enables the patriarchal systems in place more opportunities to exclude us.

Some strategies that have helped me gain entry into the system occasionally are:

- Being Participative
- Creating a Dialogue
- Encouraging Research

It is hard to show up in places where you are not invited or included. I live through it every day. With advancing technologies, I find alternative ways to engage with the same system. I train myself to think more creatively and to develop strong logical reasoning skills that make my participation known and seen. I stay participative in social media spaces. I do not shy away from respectfully expressing my disagreements or critiques. Oftentimes, this puts me on the radar of people who do not even know I exist in the ecosystem. I continue to initiate dialogues with stakeholders away from exclusive spaces through one-on-one communication, and in recent years have found some success.

India's research ecosystem that publishes on sports and related matters is literally non-existent. For the size and magnitude of the country that we are in, a negligible amount of research has been published about Indian sports. There is a widespread lack of awareness at federal and state government levels to bring science into the management and administration of sports in India. By continuing to research and publish within these spaces, I am beginning to establish a basic framework that needs years of work before we can become an equal player in the Global North research community. By choosing pathways that connect my scholar-activism to research communities, I am able to sustain a position that is gradually becoming indispensable to the growing disability sport movement in India.

Over a decade, I have learnt that to gain entry into an ecosystem that is not used to people like me, I must upskill myself with the ability to filter through communications that can weigh me down. The resistance I have faced has taught me to develop strategizing skills that add value to legal teams that take up disability sport litigation. By fielding personal attacks and political pushback to advocacy efforts, today, I am an able communicator who is able to teach at institutes of higher education in India that are looking to prepare educational leaders in physical education and sports. By choosing to work in a niche area, I have positioned myself in a space that is both lonely and rewarding. A career choice like this has allowed me the freedom to build a pioneering team for myself. Thinking beyond the average metrics of success, I am able to create lasting efforts and initiatives that will go on to change more lives than what can be envisioned at this point.

Coming from an orthodox Indian family where engineers and doctors are revered as the star children, my journey was not an easy one. The one privilege that separated me from the cultural police affecting my journey was having parents like mine who stood guard against many challenges that would have made me drop out in the early years. Despite their own struggle to learn about a completely new field of health and sports that they never knew existed, they worked hard daily to align their thinking with my efforts. They unlearnt many biases and stereotypes that they grew up with. I find joy in always saying my PhD belongs to four people: myself, my mom and dad and the community of Indians with disabilities who cheered me on.

Coming from a family of engineers and doctors who barely understood why I did what I did, I suffered from a lack of confidence to trust my abilities. The well-intended advice to colour inside the lines while I wanted to sketch did not support my growth. Despite having skills that enabled me to survive a decade of living in a foreign country, I rarely trusted my ability to shine through the dark clouds that surrounded my struggle against racism and the politics of higher education in the United States. To my younger self, I would say,

Be kind to yourself more often. Do not doubt your ability to evolve and learn new things every day. Always trust that ordinary people can achieve extraordinary things with hard work and perseverance.

CHAPTER 5
Embrace the challenge
Dr. Danielle Prescott

One of my favourite quotes comes from Richard Branson, who said, 'If somebody offers you an amazing opportunity but you are not sure you can do it, say yes – then learn how to do it later.' This quote highlights the balance between what we can control and what we cannot in our lives. While we can work towards goals that may create opportunities, some opportunities come from good fortune, like knowing the right person or being in the right place at the right time. Regardless of how an opportunity arises, it might not present itself again, so it should be seized. Learning how to make the most of that opportunity is within our control, and this mindset has guided my career.

In my career path, I've leveraged my networking and relationship-building skills to seek out opportunities. I consider myself opportunistic, always thinking about what can be created from various situations. The help I received was simply being given a chance to thrive in a male-dominated environment and demonstrate that gender is irrelevant. I like the idea of manifesting, not because it's trendy, but because it embodies determination, focus and hard work. Coupled with belief, this creates a natural drive to achieve set goals. In essence, manifesting is akin to goal setting – defining a goal and devising a plan to achieve it. This is precisely what I did.

A key lesson is that progress isn't always linear. Success often requires moving edge and overcoming hurdles to reach the final destination.

Mistakes and rejections are part of the journey; they teach us resilience and problem-solving. It's okay to make mistakes and face rejection; they are essential steps in learning and growing.

Since graduating from university 16 years ago, I've often likened my career to a train track – two parallel paths working together smoothly, except for the occasional debris that derails the journey. In essence, few things go as planned, but I've learnt that staying focused allows you to find joy in what you do. My philosophy has always been to offer my best; anything beyond that is a bonus. This mindset has driven me to demonstrate my abilities and value, hoping it will attract positive opportunities.

Reflecting on the origin of these thoughts, I attribute much to my grandma. Born to a very young mother, I developed a unique bond with my grandma, who was a constant presence in my life. Her support of my parents and her battle with a stroke that eventually paralysed her symbolized determination, strength and optimism in the face of adversity. Her example profoundly influenced my approach to personal and professional challenges. My drive to seize opportunities and do my best is rooted in the lessons I learnt from her.

Currently, my career spans two areas of interest: academia and professional football. In academia, I started as a demonstrator in sports performance analysis, a far cry from my current role as associate dean of postgraduate studies. My professional football role has significantly influenced my academic achievements by incorporating practitioner-based experiences into curriculum development and teaching, which has been well received.

In professional football, I previously worked for Manchester United as an academy scout, covering ages 12–21 for seven seasons before recently transitioning into the English FA as a talent scout in the women's game. My role at Manchester United involved weekly reporting on players within a specific region. With the FA, I feel more excited knowing my decisions impact international selections for women and girls, and it has been great to utilize my skills from the men's game in the women's game. Working in professional sports is thrilling, especially in a field I love. I felt privileged as a female in a male-dominated environment, though this privilege should perhaps be seen more as pride. The term 'privileged' reflects the surreal experience of being a successful female in an elite, male-dominated field. While some might argue against viewing gender as a privilege, it reflects the reality of being a minority in such roles within sports like football.

REFLECTING ON SUCCESS AND CHALLENGES

My proudest moment was securing the role with Manchester United. Being accepted into one of the biggest clubs in the world without any concerns or issues related to my gender felt like a significant achievement. My gender was never an issue for me in this environment, and to my knowledge, it wasn't for anyone else either. However, I did wonder why there weren't more women in similar roles. Why didn't I see other female scouts at the games I covered?

While being given an opportunity based on my skills and football knowledge shouldn't feel like something to be especially grateful for, it still does, and I'm not sure that feeling will ever change. In an industry with frequent personnel changes, I often wonder if I'll need to prove myself again. Building relationships is great, but new people with different views might make my gender a focal point. The club never expressed any issues related to gender, so perhaps my perspective is influenced by broader societal views about women in male-dominated fields.

Maintaining this role for seven seasons is beyond what I expected, given the unstable nature of football and how quickly things can change. I am one of the few female football scouts, especially within the Premier League. I am fortunate to work with a group of forward-thinking men who see beyond gender and value what I bring to the table just like anyone else. I am trusted to produce quality work, my opinions are respected and my knowledge of the game is utilized in decision-making. This demonstrates how far we have come and how I am valued. I am proud of those I worked with at Manchester United, but I am also proud of myself.

BARRIERS ON THE JOURNEY

A particularly challenging moment for me came at the very beginning of my journey in the world of football when I was rejected for a job because of my gender. I applied for a performance analysis position within the academy structure of a Premier League club in England. The role involved capturing footage, identifying KPIs, analyzing team performance and delivering feedback sessions to players. I had the right experience and commitment, and at the time, a couple of years experience in performance analysis was considered substantial. I was confident that I would be given an interview, believing my interpersonal skills would serve me well.

However, I learnt from a very reliable source that I was on the verge of being contacted for an interview until the person reviewing my application noticed my name. After that, I never heard anything further. This was very difficult to process, as I felt discriminated against and as though my chance had been taken away despite my capability to fulfil the role.

WORKING THROUGH THE CHALLENGE

Learning that I wasn't given the chance to demonstrate my capabilities simply because I'm female was a tough pill to swallow. However, I overcame this by finding something positive in the situation, which stemmed from my belief system and generally optimistic attitude. I convinced myself that if unfairness played a role, then I was never meant for that position, and I wouldn't want to work for a business that made decisions based on gender anyway. The more I reflected on the situation, the more I realized I had dodged a bullet.

While overthinking is often seen negatively, I believe I transitioned from overthinking to positively reflecting on the experience. This reflection helped me move on and seek opportunities with organizations that value me beyond gender. I knew I was better than the way I had been perceived and didn't want to waste my time on anyone who couldn't see that. A positive mindset can set you apart because it changes your outlook. I'm a firm believer that our thoughts control our behaviours: negative thoughts lead to negative actions, while positive thoughts lead to positive actions. Finding the best in a bad situation is a positive action I've relied on repeatedly. My positive outlook has also influenced how I come across in terms of confidence and approachability, which has aided my interactions with others.

LESSON LEARNT

I've learnt many lessons throughout my career, and I'm sure there will be more to come. As cliché as it sounds, a major lesson for me has been that no matter where you come from, you can achieve anything if you truly want it. My resilient mentality drives me to keep moving forward and never give up. Unfortunately, women often have to work harder to be noticed, and acknowledging this might inadvertently normalize it. However, my resilience, evident in both my personal and professional life, has been ingrained since childhood. Growing up with very little and being surrounded by others in similar situations instilled a fighting spirit in me. If I wanted something, I had to go after it; it was all on me. This mindset fosters resilience, motivation and, ultimately, success.

I measure my success by two criteria: achieving my aims and being happy. The path to success is never linear, but the challenges along the way make you better because you learn to solve problems that you previously hadn't encountered. I feel successful knowing I've given my all, seized every opportunity and maintained a positive mindset. This brings me a sense of contentment.

Another important lesson is that failure is acceptable. Everyone experiences failure, rejection or negative feedback at some point, and while it can be tough, failure is part of growth. Resilience is crucial here; imagine hearing 'No' repeatedly and then finally getting a 'Yes'. That feeling is incredible and proves that rejection by some doesn't mean rejection by all. Constant rejection can be overwhelming and lead to giving up, but I've realized that not every opportunity or situation is the right fit, and that's okay.

Knowing and being comfortable with my abilities, and understanding how they can add value, protects me from the negative aspects of rejection. It allows me to reassess if I'm truly a good fit for certain roles or companies. I've never let my gender be a reason why I can't do something or shouldn't be given a chance. As mentioned earlier, we can only manage what is within our control, and using my gender as an excuse for not achieving is something I refuse to do.

MY SUPPORT SYSTEM

Many key players have been instrumental in my journey so far, from the profound influence of my grandma and my educators to those who have set me on my current path. The most significant figure in my professional life, who unknowingly introduced me to scouting and played a crucial role in securing my previous position at Manchester United, is Micky Mellon.

I met Micky about 13 years ago when he was the manager of Fleetwood Town FC, and I began doing performance analysis for his first team. This experience allowed me to observe Micky's management style, his interactions with players and his embrace of performance analysis. This collaboration fostered a strong relationship with the team.

When Micky moved to Shrewsbury Town FC, I joined him as a consultant analyst, focussing more on opposition analysis, which further developed my skills.

Micky's next move to Tranmere Rovers brought another opportunity for me, this time focussing on first-team player recruitment. Though new to me, I enjoyed this role and saw how my analytical skills could be applied to recruitment. These experiences not only provided unique opportunities but also enhanced my CV, positioning me well for the role at Manchester United. I'm not sure if Micky realizes the pivotal role he has played in my career, but I am deeply grateful for the opportunities he offered and how they shaped my professional journey.

In recent years, key figures at Manchester United have also been instrumental. Dave Harrison, Ronnie Cusick, Josie-May Valentine, Tony Parks, Ben McFarlan, Nick Ellis and other fantastic regional scouts have been incredibly supportive. They welcomed me as a female into the fold, where I felt equally respected and valued. My contributions were seen as equal to everyone else's, and I felt welcomed, valued and safe. The respect, understanding and responsibility I experienced created a wonderful feeling of being part of a football family.

NEXT STEPS

My work with Manchester United recently concluded because I wanted to focus more on the women's side of the game and apply my academic knowledge to strategic areas of talent identification. I believe my experience in men's football adds significant value to the women's game, and my diverse experiences position me uniquely to contribute to both genders at the highest levels of football.

My academic role at UCFB will continue to evolve, and I hope to use my expertise in performance analysis, scouting and talent identification to inspire those aspiring to break into elite sports.

The message that I would give to my younger self is that things always happen for a reason, even if at the time it's difficult to understand. Never give up because it is so much better to have tried and failed than to have not tried at all. Trust in yourself; only seeking validation from others can be quite toxic, so if you can validate yourself, then you have all the power. You are your biggest cheerleader, so listen to her! Fighting your way through a male-dominated environment can be difficult, but there are a lot of male allies out there who add to your ever-growing fanbase for support and guidance.

For those who are able to promote gender balance across sports, I would encourage you to look beyond gender and see the value that each person can bring with their own perpsective and experience. Don't make gender an issue.

CHAPTER 6
'Key tools for life discipline & curiosity'

Nadmina Skeff

'Nothing in life is to be feared, it is only to be understood'

Marie Curie

I am Nadima Skeff from Brasilia, Brazil. Initially, when Dr. Amy Whitehead and Jenny Coe asked me to collaborate on this book, I was the head coach of the America FC Women's football team, a professional football team from Brazil. I recently left this position.

Previously, I have coached at the youth and collegiate levels for about eight years, and besides the coaching experience, I have also played professionally.

I would love to say that coaching football was always my dream job. However, after studying Nutrition in Brazil for three years and three more years of health science in the United States, I realized that due to my playing career, I did not have any experience in those areas for which I was getting a degree. In my senior year, after I was done playing at the collegiate level, one of the hometown youth clubs invited me to help them out by coaching on their project. My first coaching job was coaching two- to four-year-old kids. Hilariously, it was the toughest thing I have ever experienced. After that, I started to get more involved in the club. I applied for an extension of my student visa called OPT, which allowed me to work legally. The job I chose was coaching football because that was the only thing I had ever done as a job.

From that point forward, I had the opportunity to coach boys and girls from different age groups, and slowly coaching became a passion. The club that opened the door for me as a coach taught me so much about football development and how to build training sessions. At that club, we had a very special philosophy that integrated girls and boys in the same training sessions and divided them by level instead of teams and age. The same thing happened with the coaches. Besides having our team practice once or twice a week, we had sessions that integrated all staff, and the coaches were requested and matched according to their coaching ability or intention at that moment.

If you are reading this chapter, you probably know some of the struggles that female coaches have to overcome throughout their careers. As a coach, I have just started my career, but it is clear to me that the moments I have been the proudest of myself and my purpose. As women, we will be constantly tested, threading and running away from all the stereotypes that people will try to hold us to. I went to England to pursue my coaching licence; I was one of the few women in the classroom and definitely the only Brazilian. In Brazil, to pursue my coaching licence, I was in a class with 26 men and me, the only woman.

On August 1, after 18 months of working as head coach, the club decided to release me. During the meeting, the CEO mentioned that the board is asking for a 'more experienced male coach'. During the drive from the headquarters to the training centre, where I would say my goodbyes to the players and the staff, I asked myself if I was the wrong person for that role. I kept asking myself if they needed a male coach who would be tougher on the players, or a person who would make better calls during the games (Although until that moment, I did not think my game strategies were bad at all). You must understand that being a head coach is a big challenge. To be a head coach as a woman is an even bigger challenge. However, needing to change the culture of the club, making the environment less toxic for female players, making the whole club look differently at women's football (with respect), integrating the staff from the men's team with the women's team, bringing the national team head coach (Pia Sundhage) for the first time ever to visit and watch our work, fighting every day for better structure and more professionalism, asking more from the players and the whole staff, integrating all the departments, working against all the gender stereotypes that a sexist culture holds against you and, most importantly, treating all the players with respect, compassion, professionalism and high level of expectations – that is huge.

Therefore, my proudest moment was when I got fired. All my doubts about my capability and what we had created were extinguished by all the love, gratitude and appreciation from all the players and staff who made sure to tell me that they were deeply impacted, inside and outside of the field, by everything we had created. It was not a talk about how the 'female coach was so nice, nurturing, and we will miss her'; it was a talk about how much we strived, sought and fought to be better every day inside and outside the field.

I could not hold back my tears when the players told me she started reading because of me and all the author references and book recommendations we used during practice. It is important to understand that I was coaching a team where most of the players on the roster came from very humble backgrounds. Some of the comments I received after I left were about how we made our sessions a place of respect and professionalism, which gave them strength and knowledge to go back home and deal with the many issues they were facing. (Many of the players dealt with alcoholic or drug-addict parents.) That environment stimulated personal growth in all of us, and the players who were mothers would repeatedly say how much the ideas we were creating there would help educate their kids as well. The many comments were about 'believing in them', believing they could be better. Better at everything: as a person, teammate, friend and, consequently, as a player. I would never have known those things if I had not got fired.

What stands after a devastating loss, a considerable rejection or a moment of failure is how much better you have left the place. And I left that place better, even against all the odds. I tell people that I was born with a closed door in front of me, so I am used to closed doors. It does not stop me, and I will open every door if I have to. In my generation, women did not play football in Brazil. Since the moment I decided to make football part of my identity, I embraced that hurdling path as the way to go (for now).

When I was a little kid, I used to watch the Disney Channel. Once a year, they showed the Disney tournament where many girls got together to play football (soccer in this case). I was obsessed with the idea of going overseas and finding a place where I could be free to play football. This obsession took me to the United States to play at the collegiate level with a full scholarship at a university. In my house, it needed to be a full scholarship. Although my mother never asked me to stop playing football and my father would hide his frustrations about having his little girl play with a ball, neither of them was willing to make a huge investment or sacrifice towards my career. Getting a full ride was the ultimate excuse to leave and pursue my dreams. I believe they were surprised at how far I was going due to my football talent. I am glad I went to the United States. My relationship with my parents and their relationship with the idea of me playing football changed completely.

To be fair about coaching and the United States, even in the country that is the face of women's football, there are few women coaching at the highest level or holding leadership positions in significant clubs. I wanted to be a coach more than anything after I decided to stop playing, but I wanted to be free to choose where I wanted to coach, within my capabilities, and not be told where I belonged just because I am a woman. I have spent many years teaching male co-workers how to be better football coaches, only to then watch them grow in their careers with a life of possibilities in both the male and female sides of the game. Just like when I was a little kid, I practised every day with only boys. I was just as good or better than them, but they could play the games on the weekends and move on to their careers in academy teams, while I would be sitting in the stand watching them. Just because I was a woman.

I am dreaming of a time when women can go through both doors of possibilities and be judged by their true coaching capabilities. I have gone and experienced football in different places and countries with the objective of learning more and understanding better what is happening in different cultures. Myself, my beliefs and methodologies are a build-up of those moments and experiences. From what I saw and experienced as a football player and coach in the United States; my playing experience in Brazil and a personality that has the blood and smile of Brazilians; the resilience and fight while playing professionally in Denmark; the coaching licence and all the meetings I gathered in England; and everything I saw and discussed while living in Paris. I chase knowledge and network with people like it is my next graduation.

While I chased this, I realized that the highest hurdle I have been fighting is accepting that this decision has placed me into the paradox of knowledge and discernment. While in other countries I was clearly a foreigner, when I returned to my own country, I realized I was also a foreigner there. The proactivity to try to make things better and use examples from other places that embraced different strategies is sometimes it is viewed as something to be afraid of. I believe that if I were visiting a different state and trying to help my own state, it would already be difficult. Many times, I heard that my rational and direct speech is 'too American', and my detail-oriented and player-centred approach is 'too European'. Therefore, cultural barriers have been evident to me.

To constantly challenge the phrase, 'That is how it has been done here', when it serves as an excuse for an unproductive way of working has its critical moments. The closed mindset, working with people who are very oriented by fear and insecurity, can hold back many important steps for progression and players' growth. Once I heard that the question asked to the wrong person still gives you the wrong answer. That wrong person is a hurdle.

People with convictions can be scary to some people. A young female coach with convictions can be seen as a nightmare. There is something very rigid about young women with leadership abilities that is just not welcomed into the old-white-male world. People (the resistance) will try to criticize you in many ways, and if they don't understand what you are trying to say or do, they will take it as wrong. If they have never seen it, they will think it does not exist. Consequently, you become the problem. And when there is no argument at the table, what becomes an argument is random things like your look, how you speak, your experiences, your age and literally how often you smile or not.

People will just try to make you feel bad because they cannot argue with ideas. Therefore, for many moments this phrase made so much sense: 'Being early sometimes is worse than being wrong.' If people cannot see what you are trying to do or show, it is worse than being wrong about something. However, this is a hurdle we must learn how to deal with to be able to have a seat at the table's coach, because few people will have the experience you have (again, for now).

Sometimes I ask myself: Will this always be part of the game?

ARGUMENTS ABOUT TACTICS

The guy commented, 'I know how we will do the goal kick next game. We will use 3 defenders!' Then I asked, 'Nice. What about our midfielders, are they doing anything different?' The guy shouts, 'Why do you always gotta question my ideas?' I replied, 'I am just wondering if anything will change with the movement of the midfielders.' Then he shouted, 'Are you on your period? Why are you so angry?'

We lost the first match of the semi-finals. Before the next game, I opened the game plan, which the technical staff had decided on, one of the male co-workers said, 'I don't understand why don't you just kick as hard as you can and fight for the first and second ball.' I mentioned that in this game we would be more organized when it comes to strategy and that we didn't believe that putting a bunch of forwards would solve our problem. We needed to stick to our game style that we have been playing the whole year. The same guy replied in front of everyone, 'Do you think I don't understand about the tactics? What you have in age, I have in trophies.'

The away game comment

The male coach says in front of everybody, 'I heard they are putting the technical staff together in the room. Just letting you know, I sleep naked.'

The comment about the 'good-looking players'

Me being the only female coach around the technical staff, one male coach said, 'Have you seen how X looks with the new shorts? Wondering how long I need to keep my professionalism with her', followed by, 'Do you think she likes only girls?'

The 'to-go questions'

Regardless of whether I am the head coach, the assistant coach or just watching a session, if there is any opportunity to ask, it will be asked 'So do you like girls or boys?' Followed by, 'How is the locker room with that many lesbians together? I heard they shower together.' And the last one, 'Do the girls ever hit on you?'

The threatening for being a woman around male co-workers

One of the guys said, 'I told my wife I was having dinner with my co-workers, and she said, "It is okay if there are no women", so please no one take a picture with Nadima in the pic.'

Understand that the culture of football is known to have unfaithful men, and how my persona creates a threat to them.

Can she handle it?

While surrounded by male co-workers and members of different teams, one of the coaches decided to show all the vagina pics he had in one of his friends' group chats. While he was laughing and showing them to everyone, he also needed to show me and said 'is this not so ugly??? How can a vagina like this exist?' He insisted on the subject while I was clearly trying to avoid him.

While sitting at a table with four professional football players, they decided to talk about how awful it would be if their son or daughter grew up gay. After 15 minutes of homophobic comments, one of them said, 'Why are you so quiet and shy? If you are uncomfortable with conversations like this you would never be able to coach even U21 guys.' Then I started to explain to him that the conversation does not intimidate me at all, but it is hard to add anythingwhen they are clearly offering thankful prayers for what they make out to be a sin. I work in women's football, an environment where the majority of the players are homosexual and have suffered prejudice their whole lives for that. The table got quiet, and we entered the whole: 'I don't mind if my son decides to be gay; I am just relieved he is not.'

The stereotype comments

One of the members of the men's team came to watch a session, and he said, 'I watched your session. I am not used to seeing girls cursing and yelling like this. ... I don't feel comfortable seeing women acting this way.'

When a female coach is not handling a situation as people would expect, the situation becomes one of criticizing all the female coaches who have ever existed. While I was there listening, I said, 'But I am a woman, you know', to which he replied, 'But you don't count, you are different.' The generalization of a whole group of minorities according to some specific situation, and if someone does not follow that 'pattern', that person is the exception.

The quote, 'One important key to success is self-confidence. An important key to self-confidence is preparation', from Arthur Ashe summarizes the tools I used to overcome those hurdles. Unfortunately, to be part of a minority group we need to know, do and perform better than anyone else to be noticed and respected. I have a significant addiction to learning, an addiction that I started to build earlier in my life when I had to go through several resilient moments. I took the advice from John Wooden very seriously: once the opportunity arises, it is too late to prepare.

When it comes to overcoming sexist comments about women's football, I believe I try to educate myself on the subject to be better prepared to handle such comments. This will never be easy if the environment does not allow for creating a healthy discussion. However, if there is a space to talk, I must be able to plant a seed of information that would make them question their beliefs and how they convey those beliefs to people.

In my solitude, I sought to be informed as much as I could. To keep preparing myself even when I could not see where I was going. Like Sangram Vajre said, 'Being intentional is better than being brilliant', and I do not think brilliance has any space in coaching football when you are a woman. Therefore, I have to be intentional, I have to be prepared and I have to be confident.

More importantly, I can learn from books, podcasts and articles. However, sitting with someone who will spark me, who will answer questions and doubts, who will tell me things about coaching that are not put into words in a book, and who will reflect on both their situations and mine, is the greatest tool to help oneself. I have thought about this very often in the past year: the quality of your questions takes you to the right people. To overcome hurdles, you must have a trusted network to reflect with you.

There were days when I thought I was wrong for seeing as wrong and questioning all those homophobic/sexist attitudes. For many moments, I felt that this was just 'women's football' and that there was nothing I could do about it. Unfortunately, I am sure there will be moments when I still feel this way in the future. But now I have the 'right people to ask', the people whom I use as references, and the environment with which I would like to help collaborate.

KEY LESSONS

As of right now, I would highlight five key lessons I have learnt throughout my career as a football coach.

First of all, you will never please everyone; therefore, deal with rejections as if they are a gift from God. Football is a competitive sport where you compete with other teams, and within your team, you compete with other players. Head coaches need to learn how to deal with people's dissatisfaction without taking it personally.

Therefore, the second key lesson I learnt is people don't have to respect the decision, but they must respect the way the decision was made. Hence, clear communication is the best skill a coach must have. You must explain repeatedly what you believe, what you are trying to do and what you want. You cannot have unspoken expectations. I have never been a coach that tries to hide things from players or thinks that 'what the coach asks players should do', nor do I believe the same should happen with their staff. Everything must be said to be understood and then respected. I do believe in the power of constant feedback and the ability of coaches to create an environment where feedback is normal and is a tool for growth. In my sessions, coaches share their feedback about the quality and flow of the activities, and afterwards, there is a 'must feedback' moment with the players. We discuss things about the session, about what we were trying to build and do, as well as things about their lives and their moments – anything that could impact our productivity and bring them together somehow. Many times, I had other coaches or superiors doubting the necessity of this approach, using the argument that players just need to come, run and score goals. However, I learnt this lesson a long time ago, and I take this as the core of my coaching approach: to be unclear is to be unkind.

When adding up dissatisfaction and communication skills, you get to the idea of emotional intelligence and the ability to see conflict with respect and positive eyes. This can orient your whole methodology as a leader. You must know how to recognize the differences between the conflict of ideas and the conflict of ego. To be clear, a head coach must identify this first in themselves, then in their staff and players.

Fourth, understand the importance of professionalism and high demand. A lack of professionalism can easily become an act of selfishness. Be the role model of what you are asking. Usually, the team reflects its coaching staff. Before you criticize your player, look at yourself and your staff and see if all of you are the model of what you are demanding from the players.

The fifth key lesson, as John Sculley said, is 'the future belongs to those who see the possibility before it becomes obvious'. And when you are able to see more and before, be patient. Football is a political, business and competitive world. Female coaches need to learn how to embrace what is given to them so later they can pick what they want. It is important to understand that we will always challenge the status quo; therefore, resilience to the process is one of the keys to making future changes. Especially because we do not make change only for us, we make changes for all of the women who will come after us.

As I mentioned, having a supportive network is one of the key tools to handle this career. I have some people who very often enlighten me. Two of them, very special ones, are Pia Sundhage and Jonas Urias (the head coach and the U19 head coach of the Brazilian national team, respectively). Both bring their experience and intelligence to tough discussions about football and teaching at the highest level. Every single conversation I had with Pia had a huge impact on me. Learning about her struggles and her desires made me realize what could be priorities for myself as a coach.

Although both are dealing with national team issues, all the shares we had were about how to connect with the players and with our staff. The conversations with Jonas are always fantastic because we go back to the core of the sessions: how to keep Brazilian players with their passion and magic; what are the ways we can educate young players and empower female athletes. Pia always gives ideas of how things are done in Sweden, the United States and Brazil; how can we get the best of each country and culture; and the struggles of being a woman coaching in a country marked by its sexism towards football. From the times I did not know how to keep my team focused on the most important game of the year to the times I was not sure if I had the best people around me to build something special, they both always had something amazing to say and discuss.

Another person who has been a huge supporter and mentor for many years is Jeremy Aven. He taught me so much about the pedagogy of the football game and emotional intelligence in leading with other people's lives and dreams. He is the owner and main coaching figure for the club, which opened the doors for me as a new coach.

I have friends and family who give me undeniable support regardless of what level I am or where I am in this world. The players with whom I have worked with at some point in the past ten years since I started coaching somehow still make the effort to reach out and mention the impact and lessons that they still remember. That's what shapes the whole purpose and the reason for all the sacrifices that we make.

John Maxwell once said in his podcast, 'Don't let the current challenge, the current failure, or difficulty define you; let it enlighten you for the next thing.' I know the world is full of possibilities. I have many goals in my career; some of them are very ambitious, and others are very simple. Am I seeking to work at the highest level? Of course! Am I seeking to accomplish special things? Absolutely!

Like any other woman working in the professional side of football, I still have my moments covered by imposter syndrome. All the stories shared in the chapter have an Imposter Syndrome background. Being in England and being the person asking questions in the coaching licences, sitting with other male coaches and listening to their ideas and feeling like participating, being the only woman watching the men's professional team practice, sitting at a meeting table with directors and realizing I am one of the few women and the youngest person at the table always made me feel like an imposter. Even when I must answer a simple question like this one, I am still doubting my capability or if I belong in this sport and leadership position.

Consequently, instead of chasing goals and places, I have decided that the word 'Next' would be synonymous with 'more'. Next, I would like to help out more lives and somehow impact more players, go to places where I can learn even more, and be in an environment where I can share more of my ideas and receive more feedback, creating even more discussions so that we can all grow more.

Not only to my young self but to my-everyday-forever-self:

Be patient, keep working and always prepare yourself, even when you cannot quite see the reason. You do not know yet, but your discipline and your curiosity will save you repeatedly.

CHAPTER 7
'It's all about the challenges you see, the mindsets and wardrobes you choose'

Professor Stiliani 'Ani' Chroni

'Add some water to your wine!' and 'You're still young!' are killer conventions for me. Suggest them, and you trigger every cell of mine to oppose. I can't recall how many times I've been told both; early on from my mom and later from male superiors and colleagues outlining the less visible and well-hidden boundaries for what I could and should do (and be). I never liked thinned drinks (nor low-calorie foods) and accepted all that comes with my ways of being and doing. Through the years, I grew into a woman who announces loud and clear every birthday number, believing I am defying those telling me I am young. I think if some people could, they would've said to my face, 'You can't because you are a woman.' The story I will share has highs and lows and has taken me through some 'heavens and hells', as a friend coach likes to say when describing his workday.

Today, I am a full professor in sport psychology and sport coaching, though, at some point, my application for promotion from assistant to associate professor kept getting lost for more than a year. To my knowledge, the delay involved an individual holding a leadership position in the higher ranks of the academic institution where I was employed and whom I had not supported with my vote for his departmental leadership aspirations. This delay made the decision to leave home and relocate abroad a little easier. It wasn't easy at the time to accept the wrongful use of power, yet I am grateful today; incidents like this led me to new worlds and meanings.

One of the many exceptional coaches I was fortunate to meet on my research path told me, 'Once a stressor, never again a stressor.' The mediators in such cases are reflecting and learning from what hit you once, so it never throws you off balance again. Today, I am a good and fast learner, which wasn't the case in my early career. Through the years, I grasped the meaning of free will upon realizing that I always have a choice: for example, to either learn and move on or stay stuck and live the drama. I've been doing two kinds of learning: (a) how to be and do better, how to improve and deliver, and (b) how to safeguard myself, how to avoid and deal with trouble and troublemakers. In this life journey, I learnt to deal with doors being shut in my face, with publication submissions being trashed by reviewers and journal editors, with funding applications getting rejected, with team officials, coaches and parents undermining my applied work and offending me at times, with academic leaders who had no clue, no vision, nor skills for leading forward. Ken Ravizza was so right in saying, 'You can't be me, you haven't failed enough yet.' Rejections, failures, hurdles and setbacks are all parts of our lifeline, and I learnt that it's all about what I see in these, how I interpret them, the meaning I make. Early on, I used to see threats and endings, interpret many things as failures and used to hide in my shell. I would disappear for a brief time to lick my wounds and nurture my shame as I allowed work let-downs to reflect on me as a person – I wasn't good, I wasn't enough. I grew up in a judgemental environment and culture where I learnt that proving yourself is a daily deed. Eventually, through lots of reading, talking, reflecting (on, in and for), negotiating with myself (and others) and redirecting my stories, I became good at seeing challenges and delays and normalized many unpleasant events as part of growing up, of living life, of pursuing a career inside the often-toxic hegemonic masculinity of academia and sport (and native country). I gave new meaning to 'rejection' encounters which say, 'we simply want different things', whether the rejection came from paper or funding reviewers, academic jobs or board electors. At some point, I was elected to the Development Board of an international sport organization. My election was announced publicly on their website and social media, and only a month later the CEO called to tell me they made a mistake in counting votes as some came in late via postal mail. At another time, I was headhunted for a large externally funded research on diversity and inclusion matters in elite sport and cultural arts, but the offer was taken away when I asked a project manager, 'How do you expect change to happen if you haven't changed what you do' and held my ground against a male co-researcher's cultural micro-aggressions. In both incidents, I felt sad and frustrated at the start. Very quickly, I discussed the incident, context, my views, behaviours and actions with a couple of trusted colleagues before proceeding to a self-check on what I could have done differently, whether I still wanted to relate with the projects, and how such occurrences may impact my future. In both cases, the decision was to let go and move on.

Regardless of how emotionally frustrating incidents like these are, they don't ruin professional relationships with the people involved. Instead, they raise my trust-guard for future projects with them. Many years ago, I learnt from a polo player a key axiom – yes, it became an axiom for me – 'Play with the best, have dinner with your friends.' One of the greatest ever Argentine polo players had taught him that. You see, when playing polo professionally or, from my end when consulting with polo teams and player rosters, which at times change every three weeks, there's little to no time to build team unity or cohesion. Yet, tournament wins can mean big $ bonuses for the professionals and surreal prestige for the Patron of the team. As such, no matter how diverse the team roster is in personalities, mentalities and skill levels, there has to be a way forward as a team, at least for their stick-and-balling sessions, practice chukkers, pre-game team meetings and tournament matches. The way forward is to use every player's strengths and find efficient combinations between them to make the team play strong and achieve the common goal of winning games and the tournament cup. In my view, a professional environment is the space where work takes place. I go to work to develop, perform, deliver and build something. Making friends from work is an option but not a 'must'. Considering how much academics and sports people love to talk about their deeds, I decided early on to keep work and life separate, so when with friends I could live and enjoy a full life outside work.

I am a woman, a petite size one, and in case you don't know, size-ism is another real form of discrimination. In my 12 years of school life, I had to stand in the back of any line because I was short. It is very likely that I developed the skill of voice (having and using my voice) so people would hear me if they wouldn't see me. Voice is a skill! A skill which we can learn and train. I am also a feeler and a doer; I am passionate about every endeavour I put my mind into. I am honest, skilled, caring and use my voice skill for myself and to support others. 'I dream, therefore I exist' defines me, all beings and doings of mine, all my identities, and I am grateful to Mimi Murray and Bob Rotella (master's and PhD advisers, respectively) for instilling big dreams in me. I am the mom of a 23-year-old son, who is kind, caring, competent and a dreamer himself. He is fully trained on APA and the logic of research, justifications and interpretations; he reviews my papers more critically than any blind reviewer, and he's teaching me more than I could ever dream of about living a good, meaningful life. I am blessed with some of the world's best friends (and colleagues), men and women who always have my back but don't always pat my back. I was also blessed with a father who taught me by example what unconditional love and work ethic mean in everyday life and grew up with a mom who challenged me to defy the odds and barriers against me. I was married to a man who after our divorce supported avidly my career dreams with lots of help in raising our son. And I crossed paths with some great people who showed me the way and supported me in seeing, accepting and loving my flaws and finding meaning anew in trust, forgiveness, faith, hope, love and, most importantly, what letting go and moving forward mean.

I've moved a lot in this lifetime of 54 years. I've moved around most continents as a mental performance consultant and relocated my residence for my studies and academic work from Greece to the USA, back to Greece, and most recently to Norway with my son this time. Growing as a professional signified that the part of my identity which relates to what I am doing changed a bit. I transitioned from being an alpine skier to becoming an alpine coach, then a mental coach, and finally an academic. As an add-on, I got involved with the international Women in Sport Movement and eventually advocacy for women in sport became a thick layer of mine. For a long time, I identified myself with what I was doing until I came to a full stop, burned out from all that I was doing for too long, the success proofs I was seeking to make me feel good, the resisting cultures I was trying to break through as a woman developing practitioner, academic, daughter to a Greek family or single mom without caring properly for all that I am. Being on the move was my way of living life. It started as a necessity, travelling for consulting purposes or academic meetings and conferences, and eventually became a way of living life. One of the Covid-19 pandemic blessings was that I found ways to stand still and be OK. I found meaning in listening to and feeling the silence, and the way to get energized by the stillness of the moment.

Similarly, motion is apparent in my scholarship. I made a big shift in my research focus, going from conducting research on athletes to researching coaches. Topic-wise, my research interests also shifted from time to time. As I see it today, I evolved from being rather static and singular (e.g., researching self-talk and coping) to becoming more dynamic and intersectional (e.g., researching the elite athlete to coach transition, cultural silence of women victims-survivors of gender-based violence). I started with sport psychology in the early 1990s when we were still in the era of single-author publications. In recent years, I've been researching and publishing a lot jointly with a sport sociologist scholar and a sport management one; three different sets of eyes see better and unveil more meaningful knowledge. The common thread in all my research and, at the same time, the reason I shift research focus, is that any area I study emerges from challenges encountered in my applied practice or from educating future coaches. I never conceptualized a research project based on some knowledge gap identified at the end of a chapter or an article. The driving force has been the practical challenges for which we lack knowledge. As I moved through spaces and time frames, some of my challenges had to do more with understanding the context and its role. I understood early on that context is of the highest importance. You see, I learnt all about sport psychology in the USA, and when relocated to Greece, I realized that I had to revisit all my knowledge and skills as the context was particularly different. For instance, the Greeks' relational and emotional ways of thinking, deciding and acting, or the influences of the patriarchal, collectivist national culture and the excellence (at all costs) national value manifested in sport required a different approach to mental performance consulting.

I was invited to contribute to this chapter as my colleagues and book editors see a success life story in me, for which invitation I am honoured and grateful yet wish to reflect a little on what success means to me. Is success defined by titles, battles one has won, a comfortable income, one's citation index, network or one's keynote invitations? I know I have a bunch of these. I am a professor, have a solid list of publications, founded and led research groups, led transnational research projects, serve on international committees and boards, get national and international grants, consult with UNESCO and have advocated for women in sport in the big rooms of the United Nations Headquarters. I have also served as a Technical Delegate in some of the International Ski and Snowboard Federation's big alpine events. Now that I have all the above under my belt, I get keynote invitations, my research on women is cited in pivotal documents of the IOC and Council of Europe, and some of my research on coaches has helped federations of various countries develop apt programmes for their retiring Olympians who transition to coaching, and colleagues to make sense of ethics issues within their nation's Olympic sports. I was recognized as one of the 'mothers' of coaching science at the International Council for Coaching Excellence 2021 conference keynote addresses. I pioneered in building my applied practice within the elitist sport of polo, which I never played myself nor did my family – my dad's family owned a lame horse and a mule used for transportation and farming while growing up in a village during the Second World War and the Greek Civil War. Do these make me successful, a success story, a woman who succeeded in sports? In a way yes, but I think there is more that I feel good, proud and successful about than my doings and achievements, like the journey I have travelled.

So far, I see my journey as a successful one, although I got into it without a manual. I was born and raised in Greece in a family with no elite sport history but with a love for sport, at a time when master's degree programmes were not offered at my native country's sports science departments. I left for the USA to pursue a master's degree in sport psychology. I chose sport psychology because, in my sports life, I had one coach different from all the others; he taught me how to think when skiing and not only how to ski fast through the slalom gates, but I wanted to learn how to do this for others. Halfway through my master's, I realized there was more to learn and more to own, and I decided to pursue a PhD. My Graduate Record Examination scores were not good enough to attend UNCG, but Bob Rotella gave me a break and took me into the University of Virginia (UVA) programme. I met some amazing people there and made friends for life who continue to influence and inspire me, like Leslee Fisher's caring approach and Doug Newburg's life-changing resonance model of performance. I recall Doc (Bob Rotella) saying to us, 'get good at something that can afford you', and polo happened for me. UVA had an arena polo team, and the polo student-athletes attending the sport psychology class, for which I was the teaching assistant, were so good at thinking out of the box, eager to develop themselves and in their own way inspirational. Almost overnight, I decided to drop my plan of studying further alpine skiers and pursue my doctoral research on professional polo players. I didn't know a single professional player, but through the UVA poloists' contacts, I got access to a couple of pros and then things snowballed. Upon completing one of my interviews (still the longest in my life, four hours), I was invited to work with the poloist and right there a lifetime in polo started.

I moved back to Greece and started building my private practice at the time when Athens was awarded the 2004 Olympic Games, and the state was investing a lot in supporting its athletes. Meanwhile, my consulting practice with the US, UK and Argentine polo and poloists kept growing and going strong. I also started with academia as an adjunct faculty because Greeks think too highly of academics and the academic title was getting me more applied practice clients. Applied practice was my oxygen and main focus for a long time; it made me a better teacher as I had real stories to relate to the theories and techniques I was teaching. Eventually, I came at a crossroads: if I wanted to stay in academia, I would need to invest in conducting research and start taking research initiatives. I did so, yet kept the applied practice as it was feeding me with research ideas, providing real cases to work with students, giving me the oxygen I needed to breathe easily and smile and keeping my life on the move.

I was in a good place for a while until dark clouds started creeping into my academic life. These appeared when I started sharing my research findings on the sexual harassment experiences of female athletes in Greece. I'll never forget an evening phone call from a university leader ordering me to 'Fix the mess I created or else ...', following a local newspaper's attention to my research. After a six-month sabbatical at Smith College (MA, USA) and abundant support and mentoring from Carole Oglesby, Chris Shelton and Kari Fasting, I decided to look for a job outside of Greece. I loved my academic work but wanted to do it while free to research what I saw as important, without being bullied and without fear of getting fired. When my application for promotion to associate professor got lost for the third time, I had already applied for the position I hold now in Norway, and while I cried hard the day I got the news, two months later I relocated with my 13-year-old son to central Norway. The transition from Europe's south to the north has been a compelling one. I had a two-year honeymoon period in my acculturation before realities hit me hard; for many natives, acculturation meant pure assimilation and for unknown reasons to me two women (colleague and leader) hunted me down for learning Norwegian, which was not in my contract. My native language is Greek, my professional language is English, and I speak French, ski-German and polo-Spanish. I was recruited to my new institution to do research and teach in English and to help build a research culture. Learning Norwegian would mean fewer work hours, while everyone in the country speaks amazing English and communication was never an issue. This hunt lasted 3.5 years, and during this time I spent 6 months on sick leave as with this drop my life's glass overflowed; I had reached the stage of full-blown burnout with all its physical and mental symptoms. Two years later and after hard work to overcome the shame, to find and invest in self-love, self-compassion and self-care anew, I spoke up at an international panel about helpers also needing help.

Falling and getting back up became a key act in my life story. 'Falling is easy, getting back up, that's the hard part', said the narrator in the IOC video for Hermann Maier's downhill crash in the 1998 Nagano Olympic Games and the two gold medals he won a few days later. Through the years, I developed my routine: to get back up, I do a full extensive round of reflection with others and myself (what, now what, so what). When I find myself on the wrong side, I am OK to say, 'I was wrong', and change how I see, interpret and do things. You see, life is dynamic; things evolve, and I evolve, which means change is in the cards and the way forward. It also means that as I make mistakes, falling forward (not backward) and learning fast are beneficial to me and those around me. Reading (my life is science-informed), reflecting and redirecting have helped me build large repertoires of mindsets and wardrobes. In my mindset tool-bag, I have a tool that is problem-focused, another that is emotion-focused and one that is avoidance-directed. Just like the coping strategies literature, to me, these are my mindsets. For a long time, the fundamental question I was asking myself was, 'How will I grow better and stronger?' In recent years, I worked to steer away from the rather rigid high-performance narrative and added a question to my reflection asking me first, 'How will I care better for myself?' As I love clothes and shopping more than anything else, through the years, I got myself some different wardrobes to match my mindsets; like work-life values, solid friends and colleagues, knowledge, competencies, skills and networks. Looking good and trendy is all about my personal expression and not what fashion policy says, so I mix and match my mindsets and wardrobes as I see necessary and suitable for each occasion and context. While I am rather ahead in my career, I keep adding to my wardrobe; in 2019–2020, I added the NCDA/ICCE Coach Developer competencies as learning never stops, and for some time have had my eyes set on another master's degree. When I fall, to get back up, I learned to ask for help, conversing with therapists, reading the literature to understand the science behind what happened, using my skills of reflecting, negotiating with myself (revisiting my values and dreams) and redirecting the incident into one I can live with as well as reaching out to trusted friends and network for alternative views for a better present and future. I learnt that revisiting my experiential dream when I hit an obstacle or setback brings me back on track, back to my senses. You see, people may try to stop me and prevent me from living my dream, but nobody can take away the touch and feel of my experiential dream as long as I keep it alive and revisit it often. I am aware that falling has sometimes created fear and insecurity beyond my usual level of nervousness, and to keep moving forward is important to overcome the fear. Like Aksel Lund Svindal in the Blink of an Eye video, I have gotten good at 'outsmarting' myself which entails giving myself permission to be scared, to take some tasks a little easier (and/or slower), to focus on the few things I can work with and to let go of all else. It worked for Aksel skiing Beaver Creek with over 90 kilometres a year after his season-ending crash, why wouldn't it work for me when walking? Yes, regardless of where I am today in life, alpine is my safe place and safe people, the altitude, the calmness, the oxygen, the speed, the freedom, the sun, the snow and, of course, the athletes, coaches, ski patrollers, snowcat drivers, lift staff, FIS and race organizer's staff; everyone is special.

Going back to what success means for me, it can be a lot of things; the people around me, the journey am travelling, the freedom to be me, the freedom to dream how I want to touch and feel and, of course, the achievements. Success is more meaningful when it's about living authentically, growing older and better, being a good person, kindhearted, caring for others and self, touching other people and making a difference in their lives, going to bed at peace with myself and waking up next morning eager for all that awaits to be touched and felt in the day ahead. By these means, I have reached success. But am I successful every day? No, I lose focus and harmony oftentimes; I fall back to my well-known and well-practised high-performance narrative, and it's my body that sends the signals telling me to reclaim myself and meaning. You're probably thinking that I am mixing success with happiness. Indeed I am. Making meaningful choices for me (happiness) and getting to live my meaningful choices (success) are interwoven into one thing in my life. In private conversations with myself, I call this state of being and living meaning, and it has evolved to become the essence of my life.

As moving and shifting have shaped my life, regarding the part of my identity that is about who I am (without considering what I do and have achieved), I consciously worked with two major shifts: one is to let go of the high-performance narrative and finding a more peaceful, self-loving and self-caring one, and two, letting go of the need for belongingness (as defined in self-determination theory) in search of one that is more fluid and accepting of mobility, uniqueness and diversity. I grew up within family and cultural systems where performance and results mattered, judgement was ongoing and surpassing myself and others was expected on a daily basis from my mother, coaches, teachers and later superiors. I have been in situations where I felt that as my mother's daughter, I was my grades; as an athlete my national cup points; as an academic, my citation index; as a practitioner, my nonstop services to athletes and coaches; as a wife, my household duties; and as a person, my bank account, the house I lived in and the car I drove. I was seeing a lot of things through the eyes of others. I was also seeing consequences in case I failed to capitalize on these. If I didn't do well at school, I wouldn't get a chance for higher education; if I didn't publish enough, I could lose my job before getting tenure; if I wasn't available 24/7 for my clients, I wasn't a caring enough consultant. Every day was about being better, faster, more efficient, following the societal norms I grew up with, and that was a heavy load to carry on my petite-sized shoulders. Have you heard people say, 'you are only as good as your next performance'? For me, this is the epitome of the high-performance narrative that sucks the life out of the person any life between deeds as one has to have a next goal ready when crossing a finish line. In a pilot interview for my doctoral research, I interviewed Jeff Rouse, Olympic gold medallist in Atlanta in the 100 metres backstroke, and I still recall him sharing how he would set a new goal upon touching the finish wall at a swim meet. Between the Barcelona and Atlanta Olympic Games, that is, between his silver and gold individual medals, with support from Doug Newburg, Jeff found what he called 'easy power', which got him to be (and swim) at his max while using less than 100% of his power; it was a way of self-care for him. In my early 20s I was nicknamed by a friend 'compact power', which I took in as a compliment, a powerful feature of mine. I didn't know back then that my powers needed feeling, nurturing and care; otherwise, I would run out of gas eventually. Taking breaks was challenging when working year-round with different sports as a consultant; there were a couple of years when I would take off only Christmas Day and Easter Sunday – the days given off to the athletes by the coaches. As off-season breaks varied in the different sports, athletes and countries I worked with, it was difficult to get a break for myself while I was fighting for my athletes to ensure they got decent breaks to rest and refresh. During my burnout sick leave, I realized many of my mistakes in how I was thinking, being and doing, and temporarily stepped back from applied practice until I found a way to be true to myself and my clients and do as I preach. I realized also that the idea of finding a balance between work and life is very relative and can mean different things to different people at different times and places. I've also learnt that language counts and learnt to choose my words wisely to ensure they lead me forward. Accordingly, the word 'balance' feels a bit overwhelming to me, as it brings to mind a balance scale that needs to be kept even at all times. Nowadays, I choose the word 'harmony', which is more fluid, open and accepting of emerging dynamic realities.

I got to my second existential shift, that of moving away from a stricter sense of belongingness as a culmination of all my life experiences around the world, sports, academic departments and sports organizations, and all the times I felt OK yet I wasn't exactly fitting in. There have been times and places where by the standards of the context I wasn't belonging and often wasn't connecting with many people around me, but I wasn't feeling bad, less driven to be there, to work there, or less efficient in collaborating with the people at the work-table. Right there lies a commonly encountered challenge for others: to understand me, my axiom of playing with the best and having dinner with my friends, and how I don't engage in office small talks and close friendships. Similar to my consulting approach with short-lived diverse polo teams, I choose co-researchers and co-teachers for the strengths they can bring to the common cause to make it better (research projects and courses have a beginning and an end). Oftentimes we see things differently, and this makes the work more interesting and fun, the product richer, and I learn and gain a lot. Developing students is one of my job tasks that I take seriously and care for them a lot. Developing early-career colleagues is something that has to start with them and not with me pulling and pushing them forward. To me, any effort to pull and push the development of a colleague sends the indirect message of not accepting them as they are, of not seeing other strengths they possess, that they are not good or enough, and somehow, I know better. I choose to not do this to a person. This approach of mine to work, office life and people takes place in a world where belongingness and relatedness are promoted as cornerstones for success and happiness in life. My ways and rules of thumb are related to my background and experiences, and I'm aware of this. I grew up in a performance-focused, patriarchal, collectivist, judgemental culture (Greece), further developed in an even more performance-focused, elitist, individualist and again judgemental culture (USA), and now living in a development-, balance-focused, egalitarian yet still judgemental culture (but under the carpet) (Norway). I also grew up in the coach-centred discipline and strict daily regimes of sports. I have lived inside alpine ski racing and sports departments that were and still are run by men for men and had to set strict boundaries as a woman to safeguard my personal integrity. Eventually, I became a transnational versatile breed, calling home where I live and work in the world. In all honesty, I feel like a mutt, a mixed breed as I have embraced the best (for me) bits and pieces of the cultures I lived and worked in, and I see good in not being a thoroughbred. This multicultural being of mine increased my appreciation and empathy for diversity and multiplicity and strengthened my doings by making me more creative, practical and agile. Plus, it gave me friends on all continents. Very consciously I resist efforts of people and organizations to assimilate me, so we are all the same – think the same, do the same. Sameness is a scary thing for me; it means stillness, less stimulation for growth and fewer opportunities for alternative ways of thinking and doing; it is also boring and no fun. I learnt to grow and better myself through conflicting views and practices (i.e., my developmental challenges) using reflection and negotiations, and to not shy away from unbeaten paths. So, I finally came to grips with the fact that it is OK to not fit in conventionally, particularly when there is a cost associated with it, like losing myself, my values, beliefs, ways of living life and opportunities to grow. Of course, as a feeler relating to people is important, and I build strong long-lasting relationships, but I choose my people wisely and, of course, have made exceptions to my rules. In my mind, belongingness and relatedness are related yet two different concepts, and I disagree with literature that uses them interchangeably.

As I am reaching the end of my word-count allowance, I feel fully present in the here and now (what today's literature calls mindfulness), feel content, full, whole, in harmony and have no regrets. If I were to start again, I wouldn't change a thing. All heavens and hells took me places and gave me opportunities to find meaning and live the meaning I sought. If I could do it all over again, I would want my younger self to have learnt a few things earlier like,

1. Care for yourself before you care for others.
2. Care for your self-esteem before you care for your self-confidence.
3. Set your boundaries and stick to them; 'No, thank you' is a full and good answer.
4. Be true to yourself and others, use your voice and tell truths.
5. Practice trust as much as you practice other skills.
6. Don't assume goodness in all people.
7. Don't push for honesty and integrity as you won't find them in all places and people.
8. It's OK to be flawed and make mistakes – reflect and move forward.
9. It's OK to be different – accept, respect uniqueness and embrace diversity.
10. Keep the dream alive; touch and feel, love and live life.

In writing this chapter, I've been honest and forthright as I always am. There were times in my life when I wished my role models, advisers, supervisors, mentors and coaches were more open with me, wishing they had allowed me to see the full journey beneath the tip of the iceberg that is visible outside the water. I would have been more prepared and less surprised with relationships and situations going less than optimal. Possibly, I would have not felt down and alone when hitting paper and funding rejection blocks or when sports and academic politics would win over the common good and integrity.

If sharing some of my life's details helps readers see me as a plain, common person with strengths, weaknesses and flaws, who lived wins and losses, and never stopped dreaming and daring, I succeeded! As Ken Ravizza told us back in our early days, 'You can't be me, you haven't failed enough yet!'

CHAPTER 8
'Woman, life, freedom'
Dr. Shakiba Moghadam

Sport has always played an important role in my life. Growing up in a dictatorially governed country, where women were and still are seen as second-class citizens, taught me a lot of lessons very early on in life. The laws in Iran discriminate against women; women are paid significantly less than their male counterparts, excluded from certain educational opportunities and possess minimal human rights, to name just a few of the oppressive barriers Iranian women experience. Certain types of sports, for example, sports that are traditionally and historically known to be 'male-dominated' (e.g., bodybuilding) are forbidden for girls and women to partake in. In fact, sports such as boxing are illegal for women to participate in and compete in. Women were previously banned from entering sporting stadiums across Iran; however, sporting organizations are currently negotiating with the government to overturn this law. I'm grateful to have been brought up by open-minded parents who held no prejudice or rules over my participation in sports and activities I enjoyed doing, even if it meant I became an outlier.

Sport enabled me to express myself through more than just words; it taught me skills I was unaware of and brought people into my life that I otherwise wouldn't have met. But it also brought elements of unexpected trouble, where my grace and femininity were questioned as a young girl. Attending school in Iran is very restrictive; all schools are segregated into single-sex schools, where elements of your freedom are stripped away as soon as you step through the school gates. Running around and being physically active is forbidden during break time at all-girl schools. I often reflect on my childhood and the restrictions I experienced at school. One morning, during break time, my twin and I were enjoying a quick game of tag, where we'd chase each other around the school playground while our friends kept guard to ensure the staff were not watching us. Unfortunately for us, we were caught by an eagled-eye teaching assistant who stared down at us from the playground balcony. Within seconds, a wave of teachers stormed me and my twin sister, first separating us and then grabbing onto our limbs as if we were criminals on the run. They grabbed my sister's arms and legs and by force lifted her up and took her little body up the 'stairs of hell' (the stairs led to our head of year's office). I was closely behind her, screaming and crying for them to let her go. That day, after an ocean of tears, we were ordered to behave like elegant girls and were sent home from school.

Experiencing oppression at the tender age of seven taught me how to fight with all my might. Watching my mum battle her way through a tyrannical society, travelling from one gym to another to run her renowned women's fitness and yoga classes empowered me to pursue my seven-year-old goals of playing football and challenging anyone who told me I couldn't or that I shouldn't. My mum showed me and my twin how to fight the good fight, how to speak up and how to utilize sport as a tool against oppression without even having to speak. She taught us that actions speak louder than words, and sport was the catalyst to protest oppression. One year later, due to political tension in Iran, we had to flee our home and seek sanctuary in an unknown country.

SPORT IS FREEDOM

Being displaced in the United Kingdom felt alien and lonely. The first year in a UK junior school was something I'd never experienced before. Education in the United Kingdom was extremely different from my experience of learning in Iran. Despite feeling alien in a completely new environment, I felt free to learn without any consequences attached to my curiosity. Nonetheless, being unable to speak English or understand a word of English was a hard task to tackle. Much of my education in junior school comprised hand signals, drawings and playing lots of football. In fact, the only subject I felt confident in was physical education. I didn't have to worry about my lack of vocabulary; I allowed my love for sport to do the talking. Me and my twin's passion for playing football also led to some micro-level progressive changes at our junior school.

The boys at our school didn't like or enjoy the girls playing football with them; in fact, they detested when anyone interrupted their playtime. This meant that the girls had nowhere to play football, and given that I couldn't speak English, I had no way of negotiating with them. I, along with my twin sister, was left with no option but to just get on the pitch and ask for the ball. This disturbance led to some of the boys complaining to the teachers that we were ruining their game. But, simultaneously, a group of girls started to support and encourage our movement of invading the pitch. With our small army of girls, and my twin's broken English, we approached the teachers and proposed a 50/50 split of the pitch. This was the only outcome we wanted, and we were not prepared to negotiate our terms. The teachers listened attentively and reassured us that they would act upon our request. Later that week, the boys saw their beloved pitch split in half, where the girls now had their own half of the pitch to play on. Things were looking up, my English was improving, and I was being introduced to sports I'd never come across. Before I knew it, I was in secondary school, with a far better understanding of the English language and a part of so many sports teams. I felt so free.

The opportunity to continue learning and participating in sports never stopped. I tried out a plethora of sports throughout secondary school and college and started to filter through the sports that really caught my attention. Most of these sports were contact sports with high rates of injury. Despite my enduring enthusiasm for participating in these sports, there was one recurring theme. A theme that I was all too familiar with: prejudiced attitudes and behaviours directed towards young girls involved in traditionally male-dominated sports. Sports which society often labels as excessively masculine for girls and women to engage in, sports that subject a woman's identity, womanhood and femininity to scrutiny and criticism. Although I was familiar with these attitudes and they didn't derail my progress, they reinforced the notion that women are bound to the shackles of society's unrealistic expectations, no matter where we are in the world. I kept this in mind as I embarked on my journey into higher education.

FIRST STEPS INTO HIGHER EDUCATION AND BEYOND

Entering higher education was daunting at first; I didn't know what to expect. I studied for a bachelor of science honours degree in psychology. The first year of the degree flew past. I felt I was part of a very supportive community in psychology, where my enthusiasm and curiosity were encouraged and praised. The second year came around very quickly. During my second year, we had to narrow our study choices to specific areas that interested us most. This is where I discovered sport and exercise psychology. Having competed in various sports, I had always wondered how my mindset, emotions and even personality played a part in my role as an athlete. After the first few sport and exercise psychology lectures, I approached the lecturer and asked him whether I could conduct my third-year project in the area of sport and exercise psychology. He responded very warmly and advised me to gather some ideas over the summer and write up a short proposal on what area I'd like to focus on. During this period of my academic career, I also started training and competing in amateur boxing, where I later represented the university at major national and international competitions.

The summer of that year comprised immersing myself in sport and exercise psychology literature, writing my proposal and training endlessly for upcoming boxing competitions. During this summer, after a tough training session, I had a conversation with one of the coaches. We spoke about women's and girl's involvement in boxing, where I recapped some of my experiences of competing in a traditionally male-dominated sport and the sexist comments I'd heard during various competitions. We spoke about outdated views and the lack of opportunities for women boxers and our shared vision of a hopeful future for women's boxing. Soon after this discussion, I realized that I was able to merge both my passion for sport psychology and boxing together by focussing on the lived experiences of boxers for my third-year project. With this in mind, I approached my final year with much excitement.

In the first semester of my final year, we were tasked with meeting various lecturers and proposing our third-year project ideas to them, in the hope of securing our final year dissertation supervisor. I had already planned who I wanted to speak to and was quick to secure meetings. The first person I met with encouraged the proposal but noted that they did not have the necessary expertise to support the project. The second and third persons responded similarly. At this point, I was a little disheartened. I reached out to the sport psychology lecturer I'd initially spoken to, and he was quick to respond with positive feedback and agreed that he could support me, but as a second supervisor. I continued to contact various lecturers who were specialists in the research methods that aligned with my proposal. My next meeting was with a professor; I was somewhat nervous about talking to someone of his calibre. He was a very well-respected academic with what seemed like endless publications under his belt. The meeting started well; we spoke about the topic and the aims of the project. I then started discussing the project's research method. It was at this point that I was abruptly interrupted and asked, 'But why boxing?' I assumed this was an academically posed question and so I began to discuss the lack of literature pertaining to the lived experiences of boxers. However, I was interrupted again and asked the same question, to which I expressed my interest in boxing and spoke about my passion for contesting against fierce competition. Part of me was puzzled as to why the professor had steered away from the proposal. However, confusion soon turned into concern when I realized the motive behind his questioning was to provide me with unsolicited advice about my participation in boxing. It was clear he wasn't a fan of women's boxing; he continued to dismiss the proposal and questioned me about my parents' approval of boxing and whether they were worried about my 'looks being damaged' and whether my participation was in line with my culture. Despite my professionalism throughout the meeting, the questions did not stop. I felt I'd wasted my time and was wrongfully judged for my involvement and interest in boxing. Part of me felt humiliated for even thinking about this research area. I walked out of the meeting disheartened and discouraged about pursuing my research interests and meeting with other potential supervisors. I questioned why this person was so dismissive of the proposal and why they asked so many invasive questions about a project they didn't even approve of.

The next day I continued my search for my first supervisor and hoped for a less degrading experience. I decided to reach out to a social psychology lecturer. I knew her research interests were not necessarily in sport, but we had built great rapport and trust throughout my undergraduate degree, and I felt comfortable in her presence. She was so easy to speak to; her questions were professional and nonjudgmental, and she seemed excited about the potential of supervising my project. At the end of the meeting, she confirmed that she would step in as my first supervisor and expressed her enthusiasm about taking on a new dissertation topic. I walked out of the office feeling so relieved and ecstatic that I had finally managed to find a supervisor who was supportive and, most importantly, non-judgemental about my sporting career and choice of research topic. On reflection, it was at this point that I realized not all academics are necessarily professional. They can be judgemental, and despite their academic background, they can have very closed perspectives on certain topics and lack understanding of systemic issues that continue to oppress women in and out of sports.

EMBARKING ON POSTGRADUATE STUDIES

The prospect of pursuing a master's in sport and exercise psychology was nothing short of exhilarating. I was able to marry both my interests in sport and psychology into one domain and create a future for myself that was full of opportunities. As exciting as it was to study for a master's, it also presented plenty of challenges. At the time, I had just ventured into a new business endeavour and opened a small callisthenics private gym with my partner. Concerns stemming from the uncertainties of launching a new startup, combined with the realization that most of my financial savings were tied up in this venture, often left me feeling overwhelmed. Working and studying became a tough juggling act that I couldn't always keep up with; there were just never enough hours in the day, or at least that's how I felt. The inaugural year of the business and my pursuit of a master's degree passed rapidly. I was both proud of completing a demanding year and exhausted from the ever-growing pressures of co-managing a business and completing a master's degree.

After completing my master's degree, I was offered the opportunity to start lecturing part-time on some of the first-year sport and exercise psychology modules. This was an exciting opportunity as it granted me a glimpse into a potential future profession while giving me the headspace to plan for my next career move. During this period, it became increasingly evident that the sport and exercise department was predominantly male-dominated and lacked representation of people of colour, particularly women of colour. I made a conscious effort to address this in my teaching approach by diversifying my teaching content, offering reading materials and resources that represented various cultures, and teaching about how sports are perceived in different cultures. But I was still questioning the systemic make-up of such departments and started to wonder if I was the only one who felt this way.

While working as a part-time lecturer, I was offered a research assistant position to work on several projects about mental health and help-seeking behaviours. At this stage of my career, I was eagerly interested in better understanding the mental health of athletes and their attitudes towards gaining professional support and help-seeking. Over the duration of working as a part-time lecturer and a research assistant, a PhD programme was advertised focussing on the mental health literacy of women rugby players. This was an unexpected opportunity, but given my interests and my future career goals, I decided to put my best foot forward and apply for the PhD. Soon after my application, I was offered an interview. After a week's wait and suspense, I was successful in my interview and was accepted into the PhD programme. Delivering the news to my parents was one of the best feelings; they were so proud and excited for me to embark on a completely new journey. The joy in their eyes spoke far louder than words; this would have been a scarce opportunity if we were still in Iran, particularly for a woman pursuing a career in an extremely male-dominated realm of studies. But then, who knows where I would have been if we were still in Iran? A question that I often ask myself.

The prospect of pursuing a PhD in a field I was deeply passionate about filled me with boundless enthusiasm and determination. As a woman of colour in academia, I understood that this path might come with its unique set of challenges that I'd previously experienced, but I was eager to confront and overcome them. Initially, the academic landscape seemed like an open field of endless possibilities, and the idea of contributing to the world of sport and exercise psychology was exciting. However, as I had time to soak in the news, I began to reflect on my experiences from the previous years and the obstacles I'd encountered – experiences that my White male peers did not seem to encounter. Reflecting on these challenges forced me to confront the stark reality of my position in academia and spurred me to explore the intersectionality of my identity within this field, ultimately shaping the narrative of my academic journey going forward in my PhD journey.

In retrospect, starting my PhD led me to meet one of the best mentors I've had the privilege of working with. Throughout the first year of my PhD, I became very comfortable speaking to my mentor about the obstacles I'd experienced in academia, and his response was one of empathy but also advice and reflection. His approach to mentoring was honest and built on providing me with sound guidance that would propel me in my PhD and beyond – an approach that I appreciated and one that worked best for me. As time progressed, I noticed a lack of change within the department. Despite initiatives focused on inclusivity and diversity, little change had occurred. Watching from the sidelines didn't change anything; I felt helpless. I decided to volunteer my time and help set up various initiatives with other PhD students and a number of staff members to give voice to minority students within the department. The launch of the initiatives was a success, and it felt like a hole had been filled, but this feeling was short-lived. I'd hoped for an element of change within the department, even if this change started with more open and honest conversations regarding the lack of diversity and representation within the department. But I felt much of what we'd achieved was for performative measures rather than for outcomes focused on increasing departmental diversity and representation.

Throughout the years of working and studying in the department, the under-representation of female academics remained evident. Even more concerning was the apparent lack of proactive steps taken to bridge this gap. It raised questions about how students from underrepresented, marginalized groups could envision individuals who shared their backgrounds in positions of power, given that the department primarily comprised White cisgender male academics. While discussions about diversity and inclusivity were echoed frequently in departmental meetings, the absence of concrete efforts and practical solutions was blatant. This was disheartening to see; it appeared that in academia, the terms 'equality' and 'diversity' became commonly used phrases that seemed to lose some of their significance over time. I began to perceive academia as being influenced by factors like timing and personal connections, which at times appeared to favour certain individuals in securing promising positions, even when others were equally qualified and experienced for the roles.

It was at this point that I decided to step down from my position on various equality, diversity and inclusivity initiatives. Soon after this decision, I applied for a student ambassador role and was successful in being assigned as a diverse ethnicity student ambassador. The role primarily focused on working with the Student Union to improve the experiences of students from diverse ethnicities across the institution. After our initial meeting, our action plan became clear. Collectively, we'd agreed to propose and later implement a zero-tolerance policy on racism, a policy that is currently absent from numerous institutions across the UK. The policy would essentially act as a stepping stone in holding institutions accountable for following disciplinary protocols and offering students of colour a safety net if they were victims of racism. Additionally, the policy would also act as a safety net for White students if they'd witnessed racism on or off campus and wanted to report an incident privately and with confidence. The policy was set out to serve and provide a platform for all students.

As a group, we spent hours on our proposal, divided the workload and practised our pitch. The proposal was built on evidence and represented the student voice – a voice that should be represented and at the forefront of all universities. The day of our presentation finally arrived, and due to the circumstances of the COVID-19 pandemic, we conducted the meeting online. We introduced ourselves to the vice chancellor and provided an overview of our proposal. The introduction proceeded smoothly, but as we delved into the action plan, our presentation was abruptly interrupted by a firm rejection of the policy. It seemed that our proposal was considered unnecessary, with concerns raised over the risks it may entail. The risk being that the policy may offend White students through perceived targeting. This response left us stunned, prompting us to question how one person could unilaterally claim to represent the voice of hundreds of thousands of White students without their input or consent. This became a recurring question we asked ourselves long after the meeting had concluded.

Our proposal was abruptly curtailed, and the meeting ended with a sense of disappointment and diminished morale. Upon reflection, we realized that perhaps we should have been more prepared for such a response, even if it initially seemed unlikely and farfetched. But all hope was not lost. We regrouped the following week and agreed to change our course of action. As we were technically employees of the Student Union, we decided to propose the policy to students and allow the voting system to determine the outcome of the proposal. Not to our surprise, an overwhelming majority of the student votes were in favour of the policy. Consequently, the policy was accepted, passed through and implemented via the Student Union. Although this is not what we'd originally aimed for, it was still a small win for the group as we had planted the seed for future students to grow.

Unfortunately, encountering these experiences wasn't exclusive to this single incident. These micro-aggressive and, at times, aggressive behaviours continued both inside and outside of academia. From being questioned about my academic status by a male audience member during a conference to random fathers telling me, 'I wouldn't have you doing that [boxing] if you were my daughter', to being spat on and told to go back to where I came from, to being told by a male academic (who was presenting at a women in sport conference) that women should break barriers in sports, academia and the wider society by simply being 'brave' (we clearly had different definitions of bravery). Battling through these incidents is a common experience for so many marginalized communities, and even though our experiences may seem similar, they couldn't be more different due to our unique protected characteristics, how we internalize these experiences personally, and we go on to manage and dealing with them.

LESSONS LEARNT

As I reached the final leg of my PhD journey, I realized that I had to pick my battles wisely (as my PhD supervisor would frequently tell me). My PhD continued to grow in pages, and so did my experience of navigating academia. I drew strength from 'finding my people'. By this, I'm referring to finding people who shared similar values and morals to mine. People who recognized that academia is systemically flawed, a structure that is built on endless power trips, fuelled by performative measures that rarely consider the welfare and safeguarding of those who run the system day in and day out. A system that has normalized and glamorized feeling burnt-out, where a promotion or a publication is more important than self-care. A system that sugar-coats acts of racism, sexism and discrimination, and a system that can ultimately replace an academic within days. Finding my people enabled me to connect with scholars who cared for justice in this system and who wanted to make a change, just like me.

I managed to find my people through two main routes. First, I decided to step out of my realm of studies and pursue work in other areas that aligned with my interests. During my search for various academic posts, I stumbled across a cybercrime research associate position, and due to my extensive experience in research, I was successful in securing the role. This position opened my eyes to many new opportunities in a completely new field of study. Joining a social justice department was a whole new experience. My mentors were all well-known for their ongoing projects and campaigns in their respective fields. I felt so inspired and motivated to continue my pursuit of establishing a circle of scholars who were invested in social justice in and out of a sporting context.

This led to my second route of finding my people. I turned to networking events, particularly online events that were easily and readily accessible. I had built strong connections across X (formerly known as Twitter) as well as LinkedIn throughout my PhD studies. These connections eventually blossomed into collaborative partnerships in publications and organizing joint events focussing on human rights and social justice in the realm of sport. Collaboration became key in finding my people. Building trust and rapport was fundamental in collaborative work, particularly when working on pressing issues that were deemed to be controversial in academia. But with the support of my mentors as well as picking my battles wisely, I managed to form a path for myself that hadn't existed before. Of course, at times, these collaborative efforts didn't always work out, but pursuing an idea that had the potential to lead to endless opportunities for me and for others was always worth the pursuit.

WHAT'S NEXT?

I'm currently a lecturer in psychology, and I lecture on community psychology as well as sport and exercise psychology modules. I'm enjoying the diversity of my role, where I have the freedom to combine my interests within both community and sport psychology. Much of my work predominantly focusses on mental health literacy and athlete mental health, experiences of women athletes in male-dominated sports, human rights violations in sports and the experiences of marginalized communities such as refugees and asylum seekers. I'm also the co-chair of the British Psychological Society's Human Rights Advisory Group, where I've had the opportunity to work with some incredibly talented scholars across various fields of psychology. I hope to continue my work and collaborative efforts within the realm of community psychology as well as sport psychology and bring attention to marginalized and underrepresented groups both within and outside of sports. My goal in academia is to help students, the next generation of this society, build a unique set of skills that can propel them in their careers, where they can think critically, autonomously and make informed decisions that are based on evidence and compassion.

Often, I reflect back on my childhood, to the days before fleeing Iran and how helpless I felt arriving in an unknown country. If I could, I would tell my younger self to hold onto my freedom with all my might and to never stop fighting. My ultimate aspiration has always remained the same since arriving in the UK as a refugee child. Once I'm no longer exiled, and Iran is free, I'd like to return to Iran and help build a society that embraces diversity, equity and justice and offers girls and women endless opportunities in sport, physical activity, academia and so much more. Where womanhood is no longer a confinement, but a source of pride, brimming with aspirations and hopes of a promising, just future for all, and where the slogan 'Woman, Life, Freedom' serves as a stark reminder of a women-led revolution for a free Iran.

CHAPTER 9
Acorns and oak trees
Louisa Arnold

My connection to people and activity leadership started early. Dragged along by my best friend, we volunteered as Beaver Scout leaders. In our colony the youngsters, who were aged six to eight years, got to choose our leader's names based on the theme of nature.

At the time, I was rather put out that my friend was given the name fox and I was called acorn. Being named after something that fell off a tree felt quite disheartening at the age of 13. Almost 30 years on, I have finally made the connection, but I'll be handing over to Aristotle, who can put it far more eloquently than I can.

> Each human being is bred with a unique set of potentials that yearn to be fulfilled as surely as the acorn yearns to become the oak within it.

Zachary Fruhling explains that, according to Aristotle, human development can be compared to the way an acorn develops into a mighty oak tree. Just as an acorn contains the potential to grow into a fully developed oak, human beings possess an inherent potential to realize their fullest selves, provided they have the proper conditions, nurturing and environment. In Aristotle's philosophy, this idea is closely linked to his concept of *entelechy*, which refers to the realization of one's inherent purpose or end (telos). The acorn, in this analogy, represents the dunamis (potential), while the oak tree symbolizes the energeia (actualization) of that potential, a process that unfolds as the acorn develops under the right conditions (Metaphysics, 1049b-1050a). Similarly, human beings realize their fullest potential through the cultivation of virtue and living in accordance with reason (Nicomachean Ethics, Book II).

That is quite a statement, and I am far from a mighty oak, but I have certainly benefited from cultivation, nurturing and positive environments to get to where I am today. As a result, I endeavour to offer the same to all those I work or volunteer with.

SO WHO AM I?

I am Lou, because Louisa is so often mistaken for Louise. I work in sport; I coach sport, I play sport and I watch sport. Perhaps I need to broaden my horizons! I have been fortunate to work in numerous roles across the sport and physical activity landscape. I would say I'm a sports development professional, but also a tutor, coach educator, coach and club volunteer too. I am proud of working exclusively at the grassroots level in local authorities, school sport and, most recently, active partnerships.

When asked to describe myself in a job interview, I said, 'What you see is what you get' – challenged by a panel member who asked how I could possibly be like that in every situation. My response: 'Although the approach might change, I won't change who I am.'

I believe the career path I've followed, along with my volunteer coaching experiences, is almost completely aligned with who I am and the values I hold. I've rarely felt conflicted by any role I've played; perhaps that's the joy of working in this sector or the good fortune of finding a role that 'fits'.

There is a Japanese term, 'Ikigai', often referred to as 'a reason for being'. Discovering this recently struck a chord, not only with the answer to that interview question but also ultimately helping me realize why, after almost 15 years, I am still working locally to support the sport and physical activity workforce, volunteering to coach and develop netball in my district and living by the sea close to my family.

Having explored more about Ikigai and what it means to me in writing this chapter, I can truthfully say that what I have in my life right now allows these four areas to align.

What I love to do: support others to develop, be active, achieve their goals and have fun doing it.

What the world needs: more opportunities for women and girls to enjoy being active, develop their skills and connect with each other.

What I can be paid for: working within the sport and physical activity sector, supporting the recruitment, development and retention of the workforce.

What I am good at: Building relationships, connecting with care and kindness.

As with everything, there are always opportunities to evolve our thinking, especially as life moves on. The little things are actually the really big things. It feels strange to write this, as for many years I have assumed it's what everyone does, but the more people I speak to, the more I realize that what comes naturally to me is often overlooked or considered unimportant because 'it's the sport everyone is here for'.

Making connections from the start, and establishing and growing those roots, in my opinion, is essential to creating a nurturing and empowering environment.

We get regular inquiries from parents looking for netball activities for their daughters. My response will always provide as much information as possible about our sessions to put them both at ease. However, the most important question I ask straight away is, 'What is your daughter's name?' Making that connection at the start is crucial. The smile when they arrive for the first time and you welcome them by their name cuts through the anxiety straight away, just by showing that you know who they are.

THE NEXT STEP: ALWAYS USE THEIR NAME

Even if you get it wrong or mix them up with another person, keep working on it and the names will come. I confused the names of two girls for many years, only for them to start answering to the other name just to humour me. I had cracked it by the time they went off to university!

Showing people you value them enough to try and remember their name goes a long way. Make sure you check if they would prefer to be called something else; don't automatically think you can shorten their name unless you've asked first.

Growing the connection comes by taking a genuine interest in the person outside of the situation you are meeting them in. 'Person first' means learning about them, what makes them tick, what else they enjoy and what is important to them. The more you know, the easier it is to connect with them and for them to connect with you. Rather than a general 'how are you' every session, ask about something specific and remember the details they have shared with you in the past. Did they tell you something about an important event coming up, such as a birthday, holiday, work event or a new puppy? Ask about it, if you can't recall that information easily, note it down. This isn't just for coaching, by the way; I use it in all my work too! Creating a space where the little things are embedded means that when the big things happen, you have a strong connection to support people, especially in difficult situations.

The most difficult of circumstances arose 3 years after I started coaching at the netball club, when a young player, aged just 17, who, after struggling to run at pre-season training, was diagnosed with an aggressive form of bone cancer just 4 months later. Emily continued to come to training as often as she could, helping to coach younger players, supporting her teammates at matches and taking to the court with her dad at our charity morning to raise funds for the Teenage Cancer Trust.

Emily had an incredible attitude towards the situation and life itself. At times we discussed cancer, at times netball was her escape, but the most important thing was to stay connected. On a social outing to watch the Super League final in London, Emily was undergoing chemotherapy treatment. As we rushed to catch the train home, she shouted, 'It's ok, I will throw my wig at the guard if they try to leave before we get on!' Another reason why laughter is one of my favourite club values.

Sadly, Emily passed away at the age of just 20 and the club award in her memory is called the CAN Award #InspiredbyEm. It's the initials of our club, but it focuses on what CAN be done, something Emily demonstrated throughout her life.

> *'Thanks for helping me overcome my phobia of balls'* ... *not your regular Christmas card greeting but one I'll remember forever.*

Delivering a lunchtime netball session has been a highlight of my week for many years, a chance to get away from my desk and encourage others to do the same. It follows a similar pattern: the women come for many reasons, some with recent netball experience, others reliving their school days, and a few with absolutely no experience of the game at all. Everyone is welcome in our relaxed environment that fits around a lunch hour and the need to go back to work in the afternoon.

Every participant has taught me something, and I hope I have helped them along the way too. I particularly enjoyed this feedback: 'Side steps are really great to stop your toddler from escaping.' It turns out that practical netball skills are transferable in everyday life too. I am not sure I ever expected to create an alter ego for a participant so she would have the confidence to take part, though. Cajoled by her colleagues to come along, Primrose was rather nervous and tentative, especially when it came to catching the ball thrown by others. It wasn't particularly unusual for week one, so I focused on building the connection, thanked her for coming and made sure to pair her up with her colleague who I knew would take things gently.

Week two came, and Primrose returned with a smile on arrival but still tentative. Our conversation continued (thanks to the social nature of the sessions), and I discovered that there had been some bad experiences with ball sports from childhood. I can't recall the exact details, but it was a combination of being hit and hurt by a ball because she hadn't been supported in developing her catching skills. As a result, she believed she was useless at catching and had avoided any such activities for as long as she could remember.

Now, developing the confidence to catch with children is quite straightforward and part of the process when introducing the fundamental skills. On more than one occasion, I have sent a ball home with a young player who doesn't have one at home so they can grow their confidence. How do you go about it in an adult environment? I had never really had to think about it before, certainly not to the extent that someone had a phobia of balls.

Week three arrives, and so does Primrose. Obviously, something was working, and she felt confident enough to return, but how could I create conditions to cultivate and nurture that further? The conversation went a little something like this:

> *Me: It's great that you are back again this week. How can we help build your confidence in these sessions?*
> *P: Well, maybe I could imagine I am someone else for netball. Australians are always really confident in sports, aren't they?*
> *Me: Yes, they are, well, how do you feel about taking on an Australian alter ego when you come to netball?*
> *P: Hmmm, ok, I will give it a go.*
> *Me: Great, did you want to have a new name too?*
> *P: Yes, I like Kristen; she sounds like she would be a confident netballer.*

So, Primrose became Kristen every Monday lunchtime when she walked through the door. The other participants joined in, and if new people came along, she was introduced as Kristen too.

This small, creative idea really helped Primrose. I watched her confidence grow, and with that, she got more involved in the sessions and even joined in the match play, which meant catching all sorts of passes.

Coaching the person in front of you isn't easy; it can be really hard at times when you have large groups and must deliver multiple sessions. Just because it's hard doesn't mean you shouldn't do it. Remember those unique potentials in every acorn that can come alive in their own time, given the right conditions. Those positive outcomes are not only rewarding for the person themselves but for you too.

DON'T BE AFRAID TO TRY SOMETHING DIFFERENT; WHO KNOWS WHAT THEY WILL WRITE ON YOUR CHRISTMAS CARD

You can always be a cheerleader, and I completely agree with Serena Williams when she said the success of every woman should be an inspiration to another. We should raise each other up.

I recently heard about leaving the ladder down for those who follow. I prefer to think of it as a cargo climbing net, one of those great big ones you would find on the Krypton Factor obstacle course or a Tough Mudder for those who didn't experience that UK televisual treat during the 1980s. It's wider than a normal ladder so you can always encourage people to start together; it's good to have a buddy when taking your first step. There's more than one route to the top and it might not always be straightforward, and at times you just need someone by your side, supporting and steadying you until you are ready to climb again. Some of the rungs might be frayed by the people taking that route before you, so you need to take a sidestep to avoid losing your footing.

I have needed many people on that ladder to support me. I can see my head of the year waiting for my class detention to finish so I could still attend hockey practice at secondary school. I remember my dad taking me to the pub for a break and a game of darts when I was stuck with my dissertation. My mum was on the other end of the phone as I stressed about the session plans for my Level 2 coaching qualification. My coaching friends getting me through challenging situations with players and parents, generously and compassionately sharing their time and knowledge.

Being a cheerleader might be sharing a connection with someone else in your network or suggesting they join a group like the Women's Sports Collective (you really should if you haven't already). Sharing something you've been given by others, whether it's a piece of advice, an opportunity, or your time doesn't have to cost you anything, but the value to others could be priceless. Equally, it could be celebrating the success of others – not just those high-profile, award-winning moments, but the small wins that they achieve. How often do we preface something with 'I'm not very good at this but …' or 'sorry, I know it's a small thing but …'.

Why is it that we feel awkward about sharing something small that we are proud of or enjoy? Why do we feel the need to apologize? Can you be the person who says, 'it's definitely not sad, it's brilliant that you enjoy reading the rule book'? Ask questions, show interest and check in on how things are going – remember that the little things really are the big things.

Who can you encourage to take their first step on the ladder? Who stands beside you?

What you've read isn't groundbreaking or complex, but it isn't always easy, and sometimes it's overlooked (intentionally or not). To keep it simple, I've reduced it to four points and an experience that was incredibly surreal but also cool.

> **_Kindness and compassion cost nothing but are priceless to those on the receiving end._**
> **_The success of others should be a source of joy, not jealousy_**
> **_Never underestimate whom you are inspiring by being yourself._**
> **_Be true to yourself; you might end up on the radio!_**

'Just imagine you are having a conversation with a friend', as the on-air button turned red and the iconic Jenni Murray from Radio 4 Women's Hour introduced us to talk about women in coaching.

The person sitting in that famous studio was the same person who was told nine years earlier that she hadn't justified the investment in coaching development and would need to defend her approach.

Staying the course isn't always easy; you will be challenged many times, but if you are convinced it's the right thing to do because it aligns with your values, it usually is.

CHAPTER 10
'Remember that bravery is not the lack of fear but the ability to move forward in spite of fear'

Paula Dunn MBE

Throughout my time with UK Athletics, this is the quote that I always come back to. In every role I have been fortunate to get, I have always questioned myself whether I would be good enough. Fear is a good driver; it made me work harder and be better than I ever thought I could be. Despite my worries, I've always had the courage to keep moving forward, which I will always be proud of.

My name is Paula Dunn, and I'm the middle child of six children. My childhood was very much working class, but we had a very determined mother who made us believe that we could achieve anything with hard work. Growing up in a family of six was fun as a child but obviously challenging for both my parents. My parents divorced when I was 11, and I was predominantly brought up by my mum, a single parent. Growing up with four brothers and one older sister meant that we had what we needed rather than wanted. Times were definitely hard, but my mum always made sure I got one pair of spikes per year, in addition to my bus fare to attend three training sessions a week with my two younger brothers. I have an MBE and am an English former sprinter who competed in the 1988 Olympic Games in Seoul in the 100 metres, 200 metres and 4 × 100 metres relay.

One memory that sticks with me, which probably sums up my childhood and something that I have shared with my two children, is that every Saturday, we used to get a tube of Smarties from my mum to share among the five of us. We, as children, were always excited about this treat. Even though it was only a few sweets, we really loved it. My own children couldn't believe or understand the concept of sharing a small tube of Smarties between five and their response was, 'You must have been poor'. I never felt or realized we were poor at the time, but looking back, we were!

I started running at age ten while in primary school and was identified by my primary school teacher, Mr. Heald. He was a great teacher and ran all the sports clubs. Looking back, he was a great influence not just on me but other children as well, not only supporting us to believe in ourselves but also taking me and others to competitions outside school hours, including weekends. He was my first coach, though I didn't realize it at the time. He held after-school training twice a week and made sure we were ready to compete. He also encouraged me to join the athletics club after I won the Manchester Schools 75-metre race and even brought me to my first session at the club. I became a member of Trafford AC at the age of 12 in 1976, and I'm still a member today. Without Mr. Heald's early intervention and introduction to the sport, I may never have known how good I was or how much impact the sport would have on my life.

Learning how to become an athlete was a long process, and there were many ups and downs before I fully committed to training at the age of 16. Then my results started to improve. I had my first international competition at the age of 18, and during my international career, which ended in 1996, I achieved the following:

1 Olympic Games (selected for 2)
3 World Championships
3 Commonwealth Games
3 European Championships
1 European medal
4 European team medals
5 Commonwealth Games Medals
10 UK National and AAA`s Titles over 100m/200m

WORKING IN SPORT

I started working for UK Athletics in 2001 and have held a variety of roles. I predominantly worked with Junior GB teams until 2009, and from 2009, I started working on the Paralympic Programme. It was during this period that my learning and progress escalated. Between 2009 and 2012, I worked alongside Peter Eriksson, one of the best and most experienced coaches in the world, who mentored and encouraged me, making me and made me realize how good I was and how good I could become. Peter didn't believe in talking; he believed in doing. To speed up my development, after three months in the role in 2009, he sent me to the Czech Republic with a group of seated throwers. This experience forced me to learn quickly, particularly the difficulties regarding travel with wheelchair users and the difficulty with moving big pieces of equipment. Throughout this process, I got more of an understanding of the implications and restrictions of one person's disability. After watching three days of seated throws competition, I learnt the events and the nuances in each discipline.

After doing the above, I started to trust myself, my knowledge and my ability to learn quickly.

This was a high point in my career, not only working alongside Peter but also targeting home games in 2012. The success of our team in 2012 was a defining period not just for Para Athletics but also for the

Paralympic Games and movement. To be a part of it was an amazing experience.

My overriding memory from 2012 was that I told my mum and son that they would be able to get tickets on the day a month prior to the event. I was so wrong! The build-up to 2012 by Channel 4 was amazing and very innovative and garnered real excitement for the first time. Even though we were out of the country at the Holding Camp in Portugal, we could feel it. On the first day of the competition, I arrived at the stadium early for our first event, and the stadium was busy, which surprised me. As time progressed, the stadium kept getting busier and busier. By the time the first event started, the stadium was full, and it stayed that way for ten days, for both the morning and evening sessions. It was a competition that I will never forget!

> **UK Athletics 2001 to 2004: National Talent Identification Manager**
> **UK Athletics 2004 to 2006: Northwest Regional Manager**
> **UK Athletics 2006 to 2009: Northwest Talent/Regional Manager**
> **UK Athletics 2009 to 2012: Paralympic Transition Manager**
> **UK Athletics 2012 to 2022: Para Athletics Head Coach**
> **UK Athletics 2022 to 2022: GB Senior Team Leader**
> **UK Athletics 2023**
> **UK Sport 2023 – Senior Athlete Support Adviser: Head Coach Performance Programme**

I began my coaching career in 1997, and this continued until 2008. I was identified, mentored and supported by my own coach, Jim Harris.

During this period, I coached 5 GB sprinters and 1 GB athlete who went on to compete at the Commonwealth Games in 2002.

I also coached one Paralympic athlete who won a Paralympic Bronze in 2004 and a European Championship Silver in 2006.

I have held a number of GB coaching and leadership roles since 2001. It's been a long and eclectic journey, but a very enjoyable one that has taken time to develop.

- 2000 – Logistics support for World Indoor Championships in Lisbon.
- 2002, 2004 and 2006 – Team coach for the GB U20 Squad at the World Junior Championships in Jamaica, Poland and Italy.
- 2003, 2005 and 2007 – Team Leader for the U18 GB World Youth Teams in Canada, Tunisia and Poland.
- 2006 – Team England Women's Speed and Relay coach at the Commonwealth Games in Melbourne.
- 2002–2008 – Managed and led several U18 and U20 GB National Camps.
- 2009–2012 – Managed and led biannual GB Paralympic Development Camps domestically
- 2009–2012 – Managed and led the annual GB Paralympic Development camp overseas.
- 2009 and 2010 – Team Leader at IPC World Junior Championships in Dubai, United Arab Emirates.
- 2011 – Speed and Relay Lead for the IPC World Championships in New Zealand.
- 2012 – Team Leader for the IPC European Championships in the Netherlands.
- 2012 – Team GB Speed and Relay Lead, London Paralympic Games.
- 2013 – Team Leader for the IPC World Championships
- 2014 – Team Leader for the IPC European Championships
- 2015 – Team Leader for the IPC World Championships
- 2016 – Team Leader for the IPC European Championships
- 2016 – Team Leader for the 2016 Rio Games
- 2017 – Team Leader for the WPA World Championships
- 2018 – Team Leader for WPA European Championships
- 2019 – Team Leader for the WPA World Championships
- 2021 – Team Leader for the IPC European Championships
- 2021 – Team Leader for the 2020 Tokyo Games

PROUDEST MOMENT

I was appointed head coach in 2012 with the departure of my boss and mentor, which was a tough act to follow. However, I knew my work was built on the great foundations he had laid and continued the success of the programme and team through to the 2013 World Championships, 2014 European Championships and 2015 World Championships. This culminated into my proudest moment, which was leading the Para Athletics team in Rio at the 2016 Paralympic Games and achieving our highest medal count since 2000, surpassing our target in 2012. Peter taught me many lessons but the overriding ones were to be authentic, to trust myself, to give clarity about what my vision is and to be clear regarding my expectations.

PERSONAL ACHIEVEMENTS

Outside of athletics, I'm most proud of my two boys; they are my pride and joy along with my husband. My boys are aged 29 and 19. I had my first son with my first husband, and we separated when my son was two. I was a single parent until he was five. During this time, I was still competing and working full time, so life was very busy, but I had a great support network with my mum, sister and brother, so I was very fortunate.

In 1997, I went directly into coaching after retiring from competing, and the plan was to do it for six weeks, but I ended up staying for ten years as a volunteer coach, alongside working full time and bringing up my son. In 2001, after being headhunted, I decided after being headhunted to apply for a role at UK Athletics on a three-year contract. Looking back, I was definitely brave because I was now commuting to Birmingham twice a week. During this period, I was also still coaching, and yet again I had a great network of support that enabled me to do all of the above, but it was very challenging trying to balance all areas of my life. I know I was definitely out of kilter on a number of occasions when my family wasn't my priority, which was very tough. At this time, I was also managing age group GB teams, which involved overseas trips. This again was very challenging, so I had to manage my "guilt" in trying to be the best mum, partner and employee – a balancing act that was, and still is, quite challenging.

In 2002, I got engaged and had my second son. Having two children, a full-time job and being a volunteer coach was definitely a tough balancing act and, at times overwhelming. I remember distinctly missing my husband and both my sons' birthdays in one year, which was tough, but we do laugh about it now and say it was a full house, and at least I had no favourites.

Major key achievements that I'm so proud of all shaped who I am, influenced the next choices I made and had key people who supported me along the way.

- Honorary Degree from Manchester University for services to sport in 1998
- Young Mancunian of the Year 1990
- Nominated and was a top six finisher in Sports Personality of the Year 2017 in the Coach of the Year category.
- Nominated and Para Athletics was a top six finisher in Team of the Year in Sports Personality of the Year in 2017.
- MBE, services to Athletics in 2018
- Graduated from the UK Sport Elite Coach Programme 2016–2019
- A mentor on the UK Sports Female Leadership Programme, Jan 2021–June 2021
- BT Sports Woman Lifetime Award 2021

MAIN HURDLES

I sometimes think my own fears embracing different hurdles, whether they were imaginary or real is difficult to say! I was the first female head coach as well as the first black head coach, and I was a mum of two children. I was very aware that I did not want to fail or scupper any future females or people of colour being in contention for a senior role if I failed. I always felt supported by my immediate team, but I did feel I had to prove myself. No one said anything; it was just a feeling I had in the early stages of the post. It's so difficult to pinpoint, but it's just how some people make you feel, or what they are not saying.

I think in my first cycle from London 2012 to Rio 2016, my work-home life balance was out of kilter, and I was working too hard and not trusting or using my team as I should, who were highly skilled and well-qualified individuals. I was a working mother with two children, and I was aware that I wasn't doing all the things I wanted to do as a mother or partner because of my workload. As a result of this, I carried a lot of guilt and blame even though my family was fantastic and never said anything negative, but I am aware that I did miss sports days, parents' evenings and many family gatherings! I had to give myself a break and accept that not achieving perfection in all areas of my life was and is fine!

A critical moment for me was knowing that I really wanted to enjoy the journey to Tokyo and wanted the team to feel part of something special. I realized that if I didn't change my approach to leadership, I wouldn't survive the Tokyo cycle physically or emotionally, and I would probably lose good staff. I shared my concerns with the team, showed vulnerability and accepted I did things wrong the four years prior. I really focused on staff and team development, which I knew would be the best approach for everyone. I realized during the Rio cycle that, in hindsight, I was micro-managing rather than really trusting my team, which was manageable on a day-to-day basis. However, during major games, when we were living and sharing the same space for four weeks, then it became clear very quickly that it was an impossible task and I became an unintentional blocker! My change of behaviour meant that we went to Tokyo in 2021, after the hardship of two years of the pandemic, with a team that was flexible and was able to adapt to all the necessary obstacles to allow the games to take place. We didn't just survive the pandemic, as I hoped; we actually flourished, both as individuals and as a team.

Key to overcoming these hurdles

I had to trust and being true to myself and leading the team as I would want to be led! My belief is that every person in the team is equal; every member of staff has equal importance and everyone – athlete, coach or team staff –has a voice, which meant I had the tools to overcome most hurdles when they came along. I also have always had good people in my life that I can talk to, who would be honest and challenging and have the ability to refocus and put me back on track, which I will be forever grateful for.

KEY LESSONS LEARNT THROUGHOUT CAREER

Have faith in your own ability, dream big, be brave, work hard, celebrate your successes and remember that you can't say thank you enough!

It took me a long time to realize this, and it's something I've tried to do in the last few years consistently. It does matter, and it does make a difference.

Everyone has failures; it's the ability to bounce back, reflect, review, learn and move on – to try to do better – that is the important factor.

Key players and supporters

I've worked with a lot of people and been on a lot of courses, and I always try to take something away from all of them. I have, however, learnt more by interacting with key people in my life. They have been able to guide me in the right direction by giving me the confidence to believe in myself in whatever role I have been in. I would say David Dix encouraged me to apply for my first role in 2001. Without him, I wouldn't be here at UKA or have had the career I have and continue to have today.

Peter Eriksson, my ex-boss and mentor, who pushed and continues to push me to be the best I can be. Neil Black, who was my boss from 2012 to 2019, appointed me to the role of head coach and always had my back, never doubted me or my ability to do the role. Neil always messaged me daily when I was at a championship with words of wisdom or reminding me after a bad set of results to keep smiling and stay positive, which is something I always do. The athletes need to feel safe and positive, and it's my role to keep the team positive and happy despite what is happening behind the scenes.

Mike Cavendish, Maria Adey, Amanda Evans and Katie Jones have been on some or all of my journey from 2009 to 2022; they have all been great supporters, listeners and colleagues.

My family – my mum, sister, brothers and husband – provided both physical and emotional support, and without them, I wouldn't have been able to do this role or gain the success I received. I really couldn't have done it without them.

Finally, my long-time friends, whom I have known for over 45 years, base their opinion of me as a person and not as an athlete, head coach or otherwise. They are my constant and will always give me an honest opinion, even if I don't want to hear it!

What is next for Paula Dunn?

So, I stepped down from my role as Para Athletics head coach after ten years and was due to finish in my role in December 2021; my departure was been delayed until March 31, 2022.

I was offered the role of GB Senior Team Leader in 2022, which I accepted. I was super excited about the role and how it might stretch me, but I was definitely ready for this new challenge. The role commenced in April 2022 and meant I would work with our Olympic pathway athletes at the World Indoors in March 2022, World Outdoors in July 2022, the Commonwealth Games in August 2022 and finally the European Championships in August 2022. Time to enjoy my head coaches role at UK Athletics and continue to work with UK sport connecting with other sports asa athlete support advisor.

What would Paula tell her younger self if she could?

I would tell myself to have more faith in myself, trust my instincts and understand that not everyone will like or appreciate you, and that is fine. Enjoy and savour the journey because it's going to be over very quickly!

CHAPTER 11
'Develop enough courage so that you can stand up for yourself and then stand up for somebody else' –Maya Angelou

Sarah Evans

THE POWER OF ROLE MODELS

Growing up, I just wanted to be like my older brother and was the annoying little sister who followed him around everywhere. My whole family is sport mad, and I don't remember a weekend where we weren't playing or watching sport. My brother and I would spend hours out in the garden playing any and every sport. My parents always allowed me to believe that I could be anything I wanted to be, and it wasn't a question that my gender would hold me back. I remember being glued to the TV every two years when the Olympics and Commonwealth Games were on, being inspired by the incredible athletes, and something sparked inside of me, dreaming that one day I too might be able to represent my country. There wasn't a girls' football or cricket team at my primary school, so my mum helped me write a letter to the headmistress questioning this, which inevitably enabled me to play on the boys' teams. I do remember going to fixtures and hearing the murmurings of 'why do they have a girl in their team?'. There have always been small hurdles along the way, but because of the support I had around me growing up, I didn't see them as huge stumbling blocks, just opportunities for me to prove myself to people. However, I am very aware that this isn't the case for everyone, and women and girls face many barriers to simply play the sports they love. Again, there wasn't a girls' football or cricket team at my secondary school, but luckily for me, I had already followed my brother to a summer hockey camp and fallen in love with the sport.

Strong, positive role models for young women are crucial. In particular, when trying to navigate through school and puberty where we see many girls fall out of sport and physical activity, the impact of role models can't be understated. My secondary school had brilliant hockey coaches, and in my first year, the girls' 1st XI became national champions, an incredible achievement for a school with only 400 students at the time. One coach in particular had a profound impact on my career, Adele Brown, or 'Browny' as she is fondly known. Browny was playing for Slough Ladies at the time, after retiring from the GB Women's team shortly before. I remember going to watch her play in the Premier League for Slough and being in awe that my hockey coach was playing at such a high level. She saw something in me and risked a lot to pick me in the 1st XI (U18s) at the age of only 13. This belief she had in me laid such strong foundations for my confidence, something so many young girls struggle with, and something I came to wrestle with in my Senior GB career. But if it weren't for this belief she instilled in me at a young age, I would not have developed as quickly as I did.

I often get asked how important it is to be coached by females rather than males, and the reality is that the majority of my coaches were male. I think it is really important to experience all different types of coaching styles and from people with different backgrounds and life experiences. I personally think as a young girl playing hockey, my female coaches had a huge impact on me, but so too did some of the men. I have been very fortunate to have been coached by Brett Garrard, former GB Men's Captain and second-highest capped male GB hockey player of all time, for the majority of my career. His support and guidance, in particular during my years playing in the GB Women's team when he was coaching me at my home club Surbiton HC, allowed me to keep pushing and fighting for my dream of going to an Olympic Games. Having coaches like Brett and Browny, their support, knowledge and mentorship have been critical in my success as an athlete.

I have been fortunate as an international athlete to travel the world and experience different cultures. I first really got to benefit from this, however, back at school when I went on a hockey tour to South Africa at age 15. It was the first time that I had really travelled to a country where the culture was very different from that of the UK. I remember getting off the plane and driving in our coach down the motorway, with mansions on one side and a township on the other. The starkness of inequality in that first moment really struck me. That hockey tour had a profound effect on my life. I was away with my best friends for three weeks, playing the sport I loved, but more importantly, learning about the history of this beautiful country. I just couldn't believe that such atrocities had happened in my lifetime. I couldn't connect with history as a school subject; it felt like something that had happened so long ago and didn't really have much impact on my life today. But, being in South Africa, visiting Robben Island, physically standing in Nelson Mandela's cell where he spent 28 years of his life, and visiting the townships, I became consumed by the country and its history. I went on to study history at university, and my dissertation focused on sport's impact on the abolition of Apartheid. If anyone asked me what my passions were outside of sport, my answer, because of the trip to South Africa, was human rights. It was such a special and poignant moment when I received my first Senior England cap in South Africa, underneath Table Mountain, the most beautiful hockey pitch I have ever played on. I was so proud to have received my first senior cap, something I had dreamt of since I was a little girl, made all the more meaningful being in South Africa.

I was very fortunate to have progressed through the junior international hockey pathway, was selected to be part of the GB Women's Full-Time Senior Squad and was living my dream of being a professional sportsperson, playing in international tournaments all over the world. From a National Governing Body's perspective (club hockey is a different story), hockey has gender parity. The Men's and Women's squads are funded by UK Sport and Lottery funding, and both have centralized programmes where roughly 30 players of each gender are able to train full time. Due to the recent success of the female game at the last three Olympics, with the women winning a medal at each, including the historic gold medal at the Rio Olympics, the women have actually enjoyed more media and sponsorship attention than the men. However, at the club level, the men's teams are paid relatively well, whereas I have been captain of the Premier League-winning team at Surbiton for a record eight years in a row and have never received a penny from my club. In fact, for many years, I have had to pay to play.

BE THE DIFFERENCE. CREATE HISTORY. INSPIRE THE FUTURE.

One of the reasons why we were successful, particularly in Rio, was because of the work we did around team culture. The environment around the GB programme can be very intense and pressurized. Only 16 players will step out onto the pitch at the Olympics, with two travelling reserves, but 30–32 players train every day, giving their all to be selected and make it onto that plane to the Olympics. So essentially, you are competing on a daily basis against your teammates for a place in that squad; however, most teams thrive when there is cohesion and unity, so there was a possibility for the environment not to be conducive to a thriving team culture. This was understood fully by the coaching staff, and they dedicated a large portion of our time to making sure we were all pulling towards the same goal. Ultimately, it was a whole squad effort and not just the 16 who would be stepping out onto the pitch. Everyone who had contributed to training, pushing themselves to the limit was making sure that whichever 16 represented GB at the Olympics had been made their best versions and were as well prepared as they could be come game time. The work that underpinned all of this was our Vision, Values and Behaviours (VVBs).

Everything started with the Vision. We all got together as a whole playing and staff group at an activity centre called Longridge near our training base at Bisham Abbey, to have a weekend devoted to team building and the beginning of setting out our VVBs. This came off the back of finishing an incredibly disappointing 11th out of 12th at the World Cup in 2014. We all gathered in a room in one of the cabins and collectively sat down to discuss what our 'Vision' leading into Rio should be. It was important that this was set by us all as a group, and it must be emphasized that the process wasn't quick! Ultimately, we all agreed on the following vision: 'Be the difference. Create History. Inspire the Future.' We all felt very strongly that we wanted the vision to be something bigger than just winning hockey matches. We wanted something to strive towards as a collective but not something that would ever limit us. We wanted to be the difference every day; that was something you individually could control – how you trained, recovered and your professionalism. We wanted to create history, striving to win gold in every tournament and continuing to push ourselves so that even if we won, we could be consistent and do it again, making more history. Finally, we wanted to inspire the future. We wanted to be part of a legacy of women who had represented GB and connect to our history. We wanted to embrace the notion of leaving the jersey in a better place and be good role models for the next generation. It is brilliant that following on from Rio, the Tokyo and now Paris athletes have kept the same vision, which ties in beautifully with this thread about being part of something bigger, but then each squad has come up with new values and behaviours that are specific to them. It allows you to stay in touch with the history of GB Hockey while also being relevant to the current squad.

THE POWER OF OUR VOICE

Inspire the Future, as a part of our vision, was something I always took very seriously and prided ourselves on in terms of making time for the fans after the games, being humble as athletes, winning and losing with dignity, and respecting our opposition. However, as I got older and certainly towards the latter stages of my career, I really understood the power of my voice and platform as a role model to young girls and boys, and the importance of using this to push for change. As I mentioned, if anyone was to ask me about my passions outside of sport, I would always say human rights; however, it was always just that, a passion that was separate from my day-to-day life as a professional hockey player. The pandemic and George Floyd's murder allowed me time to pause and reflect both internally and on the society in which we live. For so long, I was able to simply pursue my dream of becoming an international hockey player and striving to be an Olympian, and that was my privilege. During the aftermath of George Floyd's murder, I found myself just sitting on social media, taking in all of the comments and outpouring of emotion. I wanted to look away so that I didn't feel so overwhelmed and angry, but again, that is my white privilege. I could look away if I wanted to, and I wouldn't be directly affected by racist abuse. But so many people can't. Still, too many people face microaggressions and also full-blown racism on a daily basis for something as simple as the colour of their skin. For too long, I had stayed in my lane and not done enough to question the world around me. I recognized that I could, and should, be doing more as a role model to push for change within my sport and within society as a whole.

Hockey is a predominantly white middle-class sport, played mostly in private schools where they have access to specialist coaching, equipment and astroturf pitches. Only 7% of our population in the UK attend private schools, and so we are missing a huge opportunity to widen our talent pool and find talented hockey players from all backgrounds. One argument, especially from the female side of the game, could be that the senior team has been so successful, so surely what the sport is doing is providing results. However, I would argue that yes, we have been successful with the way things have been, but how much more successful and dominant in world hockey could we be if we attracted players from all walks of life? I have had so much joy from playing sport, not just as my job, but growing up, playing with my best friends, and learning all the skills that sport gives you: leadership, teamwork, communication and understanding the power of your body. Sport is such a powerful tool; in Nelson Mandela's words, it 'has the power to change the world', and it is devastating to think that many people don't get to learn these skills or experience the joys of sport purely due to factors outside of their control.

During the pandemic, hockey, rightly so, along with many other sports, came under scrutiny for how much work it needed to do to become more diverse and inclusive. As a women's team, with the vision of inspiring the future, we knew we could do so much more to help influence the sport and society around us. We began by first looking at ourselves. What more could we do as individuals to educate ourselves, listen and then be a voice to help others? We brought in EDI experts to speak to us as a group about their personal experiences and how we could use our platform to enact change. We introduced the 'Stick It to Racism' campaign, which was taken on by GB Hockey and all the home nations, having the campaign's logo printed on our sticks, match shirts and face masks. We wanted to show externally that we do not condone racism or discrimination of any kind within our sport or within society as a whole. It was also really important to us that this wasn't just a gesture; we were backing up the campaign with action and doing the work individually and collectively to be better. At the Tokyo Olympics, the whole squad took the knee for every match, and our captain, Hollie

Pearne-Webb wore the rainbow armband, two things that had never before been done before at an Olympics. Although every member of that Tokyo squad was white, we wanted to show that although we will never understand what it is like to experience discrimination based purely on the colour of your skin, we would use our platform to fight so that no one should ever experience that or any other form of discrimination. Elite sport has its ups and downs, and I experienced my fair share of both of those throughout my career, but I am most proud of the work myself and the other women in the GB squad did to push for change within our sport and speak out for what we believe in.

Since the Stick It to Racism campaign, England Hockey has employed a full-time EDI change manager, as well as introduced an EDI Advisory Group that is independent of the governing body but advises the board on its EDI strategy and ways to be more diverse and inclusive, which I am proud to be a part of. The sport recognizes it has a long way to go, and one of the key challenges with EDI work is that it doesn't just change overnight, but they are listening and making good steps towards making the sport more accessible and inclusive for all.

During this time shortly after the pandemic, I was selected to be one of 23 athletes on the Women's Sport Trust Unlocked 2.0 programme, which also had a big influence on me finding my voice and not being afraid to speak up for what I believe in. The Women's Sport Trust is a charity that does so much to increase the visibility of women's sport, pushing for gender parity and in turn enacting societal change. I had heard of their Unlocked programme through teammates of mine and knew that I wanted to be part of the second cohort. The programme is aimed at unlocking the potential of women's sport through connecting athletes together, giving them a platform to drive change and make the most out of commercial and media opportunities. The sense of community I felt from being part of the group was immense. Everyone was so passionate about sport, but also about driving change and supporting one another. There used to be this notion that women had to step on each other to climb to the top because there were so few seats at the table, but the most special thing for me about being part of the programme was this sisterhood of women supporting one another and lifting each other up so we could all shine.

The programme included online 'hangouts' where we would get to know one another and share our athlete stories. This was also a time when athletes could share projects they were working on and collaborate together to supercharge the effect. The Women's Sport Trust also opened up their 'little black book' of contacts to us all, and they organized workshops with industry experts on ways in which we could utilize our platforms, understand how to gain sponsorship, and learn more about the media. They also paired us up with an 'activator' who works within a part of the industry that we're passionate about. For me, this was Dr. Julie Humphreys, head of diversity and inclusion at Reach Plc. Building a relationship with Julie was so impactful and came at a brilliant time for me, as I was transitioning out of elite sport and into the world of work. Julie helped me think about what career I wanted to pursue after retiring from the GB squad, understanding my key values and how important it was for these to be aligned with my next role. She also guided me through the application process, interview techniques and how to write a CV and cover letter – things I had never had to do while competing as an elite sportsperson! A testament to the relationship we built is that we still meet regularly now, 18 months after our official time together ended.

LIFE AFTER SPORT

Retiring from international hockey after 9 years as a full-time athlete, and another 10 years on top of that striving to make it as a senior athlete, could have been a daunting prospect, but they say when you know, you know. There had been a few times in my career where I questioned whether I could carry on anymore, and pretty quickly I came to the conclusion that I wasn't ready to stop. However, after the Tokyo

Olympics, I knew that I had given everything I could to my country and it was time to embark on a new chapter. Part of this was that I wanted to start a family, something I always just believed I wouldn't be able to do while competing, but it's great to see now more team sports are implementing a maternity policy for their athletes and not making the women choose between motherhood and being an elite athlete.

For as long as I can remember, the only thing I wanted to do was be an Olympian. That was always my main goal. I did work experience, completed workshops and participated in programmes designed to help athletes transition out of sports while I was competing, but I never really knew what I wanted to do as a job. Before the pandemic, my business plan for after retirement was to set up a doggie daycare business in my local area! However, the EDI work I have mentioned gave me such energy and a sense of purpose that I knew that my next career needed to be aligned with two of my core values: helping people and sport. Through the Women's Sport Trust's Unlocked programme, I had the opportunity to speak at a Leaders in Sport Diversity Forum on Women's Sport in November 2021. It was a great chance to speak about my experiences to the wider sports community and make connections while there. Three months later, I saw a job advert on LinkedIn from Leaders, and although I didn't know too much about the specific role, I knew that they as a company were aligned with my values. You never know what opportunities will come out of meeting someone, networking or attending an event, so it's important to put yourself out there and seize any opportunity you can. I joined the Leaders team in March 2022 and was excited for my new chapter after elite sport. Leaders in Sport connects the most influential people in sport to the most powerful ideas, and I love being able to be part of the sports industry and still be at the forefront of change. A lot of my role is working with performance practitioners within elite sport and helping them with their professional development. We have a membership of elite sports practitioners, coaches and decision makers, and due to the nature of the elite sport, where historically these jobs have been occupied by men, there was a distinct lack of female representation within our membership. Therefore, what could we as a company do to help the sports industry progress and become more inclusive for women? How could we use our network to help amplify the amazing work so many women are already doing in this field and show a pathway to aspiring women that these roles are also available for them? We have launched a Women's High-performance Sport Community Group for anyone working within a performance role at an elite women's sports team, any female working within men's elite sport or also any male allies. We wanted to create an action-oriented space for those working in high-performance sport who are passionate about growing women's sport and access for women, to learn, build relationships, solve shared problems and share those learnings with the wider performance community. There are still so many barriers for women, be it as athletes or within a working capacity. We still have a very long way to go, but I'm always filled with energy and enthusiasm when you can get together with others who are passionate about making change in this area and working together to uplift one another.

Having people in your life who can help shape and guide you as you grow and transition into different phases of your life is incredibly important. I'm so grateful for the guidance and support I have received throughout these different phases and have felt so empowered by the number of strong women who take the time to lift up others around them. Emma Mitchell, our performance lifestyle adviser at GB Hockey, is another crucial figure for me. She was there to support and guide me throughout my playing career, whether through injury, non-selection or retirement, and was hugely impactful in my smooth transition into life after professional sport. Finally, the support from my family cannot be overstated. Being an elite sportsperson is tremendously hard, and you have to make sacrifices in order to achieve your dreams. But what often gets overlooked is that your family and loved ones also have to buy into these sacrifices. They go through the rollercoaster of emotions that you do and have no control over the outcome. I am hugely grateful for the support and love I have always had from both of my parents and the values they instilled in me from an early age. My dad, a lawyer, constantly reinforced that everyone should be treated fairly and equitably, and my mum, a psychotherapist who would always help me understand that you cannot judge someone unless you have walked in their shoes, which of course, you can never do! My husband, Scott, was the one to pick me up after every setback and help me piece myself back together. He was the one who had to put up with my schedule and have everything planned around it, even having to change our wedding date as it clashed with the World Cup! Finally, my daughter Maya; I have always been a fierce promoter of women's sport, and these feelings have only been amplified since the arrival of our daughter. I hope that her path and her generation of girls' paths will come to know sport as an inclusive environment in which to thrive.

Having a solid support system is crucial for an elite sportsperson, but it's also crucial for anyone. Being able to speak about your emotions, having people to love, guide and challenge you is so important, and allowing young girls and boys to have these role models and support systems from an early age is one of the most important things we can do to help them be successful.

CHAPTER **12**
'You can't play rugby, it's a boy's sport'
Dr. Amy Whitehead

Why can't I?

> *'You can't play rugby, it's a boy's sport.'*
> *'Women should be in the kitchen.'*

This is what My dad would often say, and that was the rhetoric that I grew up around, but I always wondered why this was such a thing. Growing up, both my parents worked, meaning I was often stuck with my two older brothers, following them around and trying to make myself a useful member of their football, basketball or tag team (or any sport they would allow me to join in with). I would watch my grandmothers (Nanas) cook for my grandads every day and watch them fuss over them. Don't get me wrong, if they're happy to do this, then I'm happy for them, but something just didn't sit right with me from such a young age. As a child, I would always question why I couldn't be in the football and rugby team – 'no girls allowed' – or 'it's too dangerous for you, Amy'. I would be baffled at the difference in Christmas presents that I would receive in comparison to my brothers – they were bought skateboards and cool-looking bikes, and I was always given dolls and much more feminine gifts. I'd hear things like, 'girls should be polite, kind and caring'…Hang on a minute… shouldn't everyone?

Career-wise, growing up in an extremely white working-class town in the North of England (Barrow-in-Furness) meant that working-class traditions were prevalent (they still are). Men go to work in the 'shipyard' or sign up for some sort of manual labour apprenticeship and the women … well, the women don't really get a thought, or they certainly didn't when I was growing up. The lack of career discussion or the assumption that women can't do 'male'-oriented work was and still occurs today. Can you tell this is something that bothered me?!

Don't get me wrong, my parents and my grandparents were amazing in many ways. They were super loving and fully supported my more gender-appropriate sports (e.g., tennis, netball and hockey), always driving me to practice, funding my coaching (as a tennis player) and supporting me to become a coach in my teens. This provided me with the opportunity to compete for my county and, as a result, allowed me to see different places in the country, socialize with people of different social classes and understand that there was so much more to see outside of my little town. I saw how other players were attending university, studying really cool topics and telling tales of independence. I realized then that this was what I'd been waiting for, a way to spread my wings and move into the big, wide world of university life.

'WHAT THE HECK IS SPORT PSYCHOLOGY?'

As previously mentioned, I come from a pretty 'traditional' environment, so you can imagine that when I tell my parents that I'd like to study sport psychology, the response I get is, 'What the heck is that?' During my A-levels I was drawn to psychology, understanding human behaviour and how the social environment affects how we think and behave. However, my true love is, and always has been, sport. Sport gave me freedom; it gave me joy and happiness, but it also gave me frustration, anger and upset. As a county tennis player, I loved the sport, but it would also leave me enraged when I would choke under pressure during most competitive matches. It would always leave me questioning why I couldn't perform in the competition like I was playing during practice. And there grew the marriage of sport and psychology for me, and my quest to become a sport psychologist.

Now this was in 2004 – and it wasn't only my parents asking 'what the heck is sport psychology'. Most people around me were asking the same question, and although there were only two universities in the country at the time that offered this type of course – I knew it was something that I was going to pursue.

Moral of this point: follow your passion!

Fast forward to 2008, I'd finished my undergraduate degree in sport psychology and had just completed my master's programme in sport and exercise psychology from the University of Central Lancashire in Preston, UK (UCLan). I'd spent most of my time during my studies playing tennis, national league basketball (picked this up after the demise of my tennis career) and coaching tennis on evenings and weekends (something had to fund my nights out). At this point, sport psychologist roles were difficult to come by. The profession was still very much in its infancy in terms of requiring an official qualification and the 'cowboy/girl/person' culture still existed. By this, I mean that a lot of people were calling themselves sport psychologists or performance psychologists, mental coaches, etc., without any formal qualifications. The British Psychological Society had a supervised practice route to become a fully fledged Health Care and Practitioner Council (HCPC) certified sport and exercise psychologist, but it was still early days and there were so many people calling themselves 'sport and exercise psychologists' without even an undergraduate degree. At 21, jobless and floating around in Preston, picking up some tennis coaching hours and waitressing work, I decided to do what every other clueless 21-year-old straight out of studies did. I buried my head in the sand and decided to visit my friend Mike at his home in Sacramento, California. After all, what else is a penniless graduate student to do?! And as a penniless graduate, yes I did have to go back to my dad who questioned my university choices (and almost told me 'I told you so') and ask him to fund said 'jolly/soul searching' trip – which he very kindly did.

It's not just what you know, it's who you know.

During my time in California, visiting my friend Mike (we both studied MSc sport psychology modules together), I received an email from my university basketball coach, Craig. Craig was also a lecturer on the BSc sport coaching programme at UCLan, and at the time they were in need of someone with sport psychology expertise to contribute to their degree programme. This was the beginning of my journey into the application of sport psychology in coaching. I didn't and couldn't see it then, but my love and motivation for coaching, combined with the knowledge of sport and exercise psychology that I had gained throughout my studies, created a pathway for me into the world of academia and allowed me to combine my practical experience of coaching with the world of sport psychology.

I want to take a minute here to recognize the team at UCLan, specifically Dr. Craig Wright and Brian Jones, for giving me this opportunity. I explained earlier in this chapter some of the implicit (and explicit) barriers I felt as a female, but at no point did I ever feel any of these invisible barriers holding me back. Although I am fully aware of the many barriers women still face in academia and the gender gaps (pay and roles), all I felt at the time was support and encouragement. To supplement that, I had other female academics embarking on this journey alongside me (e.g., Dr. Danielle Prescott), and we had a fantastic team at UCLan.

NO OPPORTUNITY IS A WASTED OPPORTUNITY

Was it the motivation to prove them wrong? Was it the motivation to make them proud? Or was it just the thought that anything is now possible? I can't say for sure, but maybe it was a combination of all three of these questions. At 22, my step into academia was the most scary and exciting opportunity. Teaching students, some were my age or older, was terrifying. I would sweat profusely with anxiety and stumble over my words. But I came to realize that students (and people in general) can be really understanding and supportive. Some students could tell I was nervous, but they equally respected where I was coming from and allowed me to move through the stages of learning to become a lecturer. One of the best lessons I learnt was from a teaching observation, where a colleague said to me, 'you don't have to vomit information onto the students, you just need to help facilitate their learning' – this was a light bulb moment for me. No longer did I have to spend hours and hours pouring information into my lecture slides; I now developed the art of understanding the people in front of me and being confident enough to bring them into the conversation. I guess this was also a life lesson that helped me with my work in sport psychology. As I was early into my training as a sport and exercise psychologist, I started to also understand the importance of 'supporting' clients on their journey rather than feeling the need to pour information into them.

'Amy, do you want to go to Spain to teach students about the psychology of training?' Err yes! 'Amy, do you want to take some students to Zambia to coach children and learn about the culture?' Yes! 'Amy, do you want to help develop volunteers for the 2014 Winter Olympics in Sochi, Russia?' Yes! 'Amy, we'd like you to do a PhD, can we fund and support you to do this?' Yes, yes, yes! As a 22/23-year-old, the way I looked at it, my initiation into academia was full to the brim with opportunities. Now don't get me wrong, I worked long hours, I was teaching a lot of hours (trying to impress), starting a PhD and still coaching and playing national league basketball most evenings and weekends – but I was so grateful for these opportunities, that it was all totally worth it.

So, the dual PhD and lecturing journey began. I think doing a PhD part-time and working as a full-time lecturer was the best lesson in time management and resilience. Hats off to those people who do both with a family. Lecturing or working full time and doing a PhD is like constantly having a monkey on your back; it's always there. You finish a day of lectures, and it's there shouting, 'Amy, come on, get cracking.'

Following my passion was definitely something I took into my PhD, and I have my supervisors, Professor Remco Polman and Dr. Jamie Taylor, to thank for giving me creative freedom while providing the definition of an autonomy-supportive relationship. Remco, being an absolute legend in the field of sport psychology, provided me with the initial guidance and direction, and Jamie was my absolute rock whenever I needed him. Both of them were available when I needed them but would allow me to disappear for weeks (sometimes even months) when I was taking a deep dive into reading or working out how to tackle my data analysis. I felt a mutual trust between us, and this is something that I hope to take into my own supervision.

My PhD topic has also become a big part of who I am as a researcher. As previously mentioned, I'm fascinated by how people think and how decisions are made, and what better way to understand this information than to ask them to verbalize everything they are thinking as they are performing. And there grew my obsession with the 'Think Aloud' method and applying this method to every possible scenario: athletes, coaches, medical professionals, etc.

IT WASN'T ALL SUNSHINE AND ROSES

Yes, I was having the time of my life, feeling extremely grateful for all of the opportunities I was offered, but I wanted to share with you an early experience and lesson I learnt. I don't want to paint everything as rosy, as I was a young female working in a male-oriented environment. There would be times when something just didn't feel right inside me; I couldn't quite put my finger on it at the time, but as I reflect back, I have a much clearer view of what was happening.

At 26, I secured my first part-time, long-term(ish), paid sport psychology role within a football club. I won't name the club, but said club had just been taken over by a very wealthy owner, and as a result, they were able to improve their sport science provision. One area they sought to improve was the psychology department. This was a big deal at the time; football clubs still didn't take sport psychology seriously, and most of the people they hired were ex (male) players who claimed to be 'mental performance' experts. I was (again) nervous but excited at the same time. I'd been recommended by a colleague who knew the manager, and they wanted to meet with me to discuss how I could support the club. My first meeting was with the manager and head coach. Both were very nice, but when I asked what they were looking for support with, their response was, 'Well, what can you do for us? What does a sport psychologist do?' This was a great first lesson in being more prepared for these types of meetings and helped me to consider how I set up expectations of how I can provide support as a sport psychologist to a team and individuals moving forward.

This role came with highs and lows. The highs involved the buzz I would get from providing support to great players who bought into the work I was trying to implement and seeing them succeed in the league. The lows, however, involved feeling like a constant imposter. As the only female in the whole coaching staff, I experienced a whole host of sexism. From what I would consider minor issues, such as having to share a disgusting toilet with the men (as many grounds didn't have a female toilet), being kitted out with ridiculously big men's sized kits because they didn't have or couldn't be bothered to order me kit that actually fit, to more serious incidents, where a coach thought it acceptable to grab my arse and pass it off as 'banter', to asking if they could see pictures of my female partner because they wanted to know if she was 'fit'. At the time, being young and naïve, I just thought that was the norm – something that women just had to put up with. However, of course, I now realize that this doesn't have to be the case. This is something that I constantly stress to my trainees. Speaking up and calling out this behaviour may feel like career-ending behaviour, but if we don't challenge this now, then how are things supposed to change for women working in these environments? Something I wish I could have told my younger self.

As a practitioner, I have now been able to grow confident in understanding my 'non negotiables', to understand what I won't accept, and how to challenge these. I seek environments where I feel I am able to work in congruence with my philosophy. Don't get me wrong, this doesn't mean I shy away from difficult environments; it just means that I will outline my expectations, call out unjust behaviour, and if I feel I am in an unsafe or threatening environment, I will remove myself from it. I know my worth!

These experiences have also fuelled my fire to work and research in the area of sexism within sport. I've been fortunate to supervise an outstanding professional doctorate student Dr. Kristin McGinty-Minister who is leading some fabulous and important research that focusses on women's experiences of sexism when working in sporting careers (supported by Dr. Laura Swettenham and Dr. Francesca Champ).

'FIND A JOB THAT YOU ENJOY, AND YOU WILL NEVER WORK A DAY IN YOUR LIFE'

This is something that sounds totally cliché, but it's genuinely how I feel.

In 2015, I completed my PhD and knew I had a thirst for research. To develop myself in this area, I knew moving to a high-performing research institution was important. This is when I decided to make the jump from my comfortable UCLan family to one of the highest-performing sport science departments in the UK (number six in the world at the time of this chapter), Liverpool John Moores University (LJMU).

Over the last ten years, I have been supported by many fantastic colleagues and managers who have assisted me in my journey to Association Professor (Reader) in sport psychology and coaching. I'm honoured to lead the coaching and pedagogy research group within the Research Institute of Sport and Exercise Sciences, and I have been a manager for nine amazing colleagues within our sport coaching bachelors programme. During this time, I have also secured Health Care and Practitioner Council (HCPC) accreditation as a sport and exercise psychologist, and I run my own sport psychology consultancy, where I offer sport psychology support to athletes, coaches and organizations. Don't get me wrong, this hasn't been a breeze; I've experienced more 'bum grabbing' from a male colleague (this was challenged and reported), male professors trying to take credit for my work (this was also challenged, and said professor apologized – victory!), I've had promotion rejections (always a learning process) and made many mistakes along the way. However, having said that, I still can't deny the smile on my face when someone asks me about my work, and I beam with pride (and bore the pants off them) when I go into (what I think are) the fascinating insights into the varied and interesting work that I do. I also can't forget that I am surrounded by people who challenge me on a daily basis, stretch my mind and change my perspectives on all sorts of ideas.

My colleagues in academia can be cutthroat and at times harsh critics, but the harshness is a reason why they are so successful. They are sharp, critical and are always throwing challenging questions into the mix. Whether this is regarding how we deliver the content and teach the way we do, how we conduct research or how we approach applied practice. Don't be afraid of conflict or challenge – when done in a safe space, it is what helps you grow. This is why I believe I work in one of the most successful sport science departments in the world. We never settle for OK; we push for the best. Not only my colleagues at LJMU but also my colleagues outside my institution – in academia and the world of applied sport psychology. As I mention further on, you get to find 'your people' who support you and make your job even more fulfilling.

> My students: Being able to have weekly discussions with students about how they see the world is super enjoyable and a privilege. Working with PhD students who are at the forefront of their research area, and who bring new ideas to the table, constantly keeps me on my toes and pushes me to learn more in order to be a better supervisor.

My trainees: As a supervisor for trainee sport and exercise psychologists on their way to being HCPC accredited, I feel extremely honoured to be trusted to guide and support these individuals. Whether this is on the professional doctorate route at LJMU or via the BASES SEPAR programme, the level of energy and ideas I get from this role is unbelievable. Special mention to my amazing friend and co-editor Jenny Coe, who is also one of these trainees, doing fantastic things and very soon to be a qualified HCPC Sport and Exercise Psychologist.

As a practitioner sport psychologist, my clients are phenomenal individuals who trust me with their thoughts and feelings and share their insecurities and views of the world. I am in constant awe of the many people I get to meet in this role and get a glimpse into their world. Clients come to me for support; sometimes they express feelings of weakness or a lack of confidence; however, what they don't realize is the strength they have to seek support in the first place, and nothing is more rewarding than helping them see that.

FIND YOUR PEOPLE

Now, at the age of 38, as a gay woman with a mixed-race wife, I guess I have really started to make sense of why I never felt that I fit into my home environment growing up. I now know that leaving home at 18 was about finding 'my people'. That doesn't mean that my family (and my friends who still today are my biggest supporters) are not my people, but at the time my current environment felt stifling. I felt like I couldn't be myself, and I was unable to grow in a way that suited me. Over the years, I have met some great people and not-so-great people, but what I have learnt is that just because you may be within a certain environment or organization that doesn't mean that's where 'your people' are. If you don't feel like you are surrounded by the right people, go and find 'your people'. Find people that challenge you but in a safe and supportive way, find people that want the best for you, find people that stick with you even when you are not the best version of yourself. These are my people, from my wife who sits next to me right now, to my friends and colleagues halfway across the world.

And people can change! Don't get me wrong, I still have challenging conversations with my family, but I can't fault them for being open to learning. They ask questions, they listen and most of the time they change their behaviours. They are kind, they want to understand me and they want to try and understand people who are not like them. Just because we don't always see the world in the same way, doesn't mean they aren't 'my people'. This is why I love psychology!

FINALLY, HARD WORK BEATS TALENT WHEN TALENT DOESN'T WORK HARD

'You're not that bright, Amy, but you try really hard.' This is something my mum still says to me. I used to get offended, but after studying expertise and skill development, I finally understood. I do wonder how ingrained it has become over the years. Stolen from a Nike advert, 'Hard work beats talent when talent doesn't work hard.' This is something that always stays with me; I may not have been the sharpest tool in the box, but I understand the importance of taking opportunities and working hard. Is this because I feel as a woman that I should take as many opportunities as possible and feel grateful for them? I don't know. Is it because I felt that these types of opportunities were not for women like me? I'm not sure. Regardless, I'm actually happy to have this mindset. Don't get me wrong, I completely appreciate that some people experience more opportunities than others; I totally accept this. I understand that I have certain privileges over others, and my experiences have been a result of my privileges (e.g., being a white woman in a Western society). However, I also hope that readers can take their own interpretations from this chapter.

CHAPTER 13
Questioning the Norms, Encouraging Change, and Strengthening the Path

Jen Coe

Sport has been the foundation of my life for many decades. In this chapter, I aim to share the stories from my journey – the triumphs, the trials and the transformative moments. Along the way, I've met remarkable people in extraordinary places, but I've also faced the darker side of the sporting world, where people lack self-awareness, empathy and kindness. While I don't want this chapter to dwell solely on the negatives, it's essential to acknowledge the persistent sexism and inequality that have peppered my experiences and the resilience I have built up in navigating which moments to fight against. Sport has provided me with incredible opportunities to excel, yet it has also, at times, undermined my confidence.

I've often placed myself in challenging situations to grow, but these experiences have sometimes come with unintended consequences such as sexism, xenophobia, loneliness and blows to my self-worth. However, there have also been golden moments of connection, success and pure inspiration, offering hope for progress for women in sport. I am committed to continuing this journey and being unapologetically myself as I 'feel the fear and do it anyway.'

Reflecting on my journey and the various roles I've assumed in the sporting landscape, certain themes and challenges stand out. My two brilliant sisters and I were fortunate to grow up in a household that encouraged us to pursue any interests we liked. Despite some traditional mindsets, all three of us have achieved significant success as women in sport and in our respective fields. I have tried to be a role model as the older sister over the years, but at times they are the ones mentoring me through life's different challenges. I still find it interesting that, at the top of their fields in the corporate and teaching worlds, we all still encounter similar experiences in different ways. I also have to acknowledge how different policies and ways of working can help prevent or dilute the frequency and intensity of these occurrences.

I consider myself a confident person, having built this confidence over time. Yet, the daily reminders on social media of women's struggles, coupled with frequent stories of inequality in various sports environments, make it difficult to move past these issues. There is still much work to be done, and for a while longer, I need to be ready to face these challenges head-on and support others to do the same. At times I have asked myself, 'Is it me? Am I too assertive and coming on too strong? Am I not clear enough, is it my accent?' On many occasions I've shared some insight in a room, and a man in the workshop will then share the exact same observation and get a favourable response. While it would be easy to attribute everything to gender, I've learnt to reflect more deeply to navigate these experiences, and overtime, I have become more attuned to my thoughts, feelings and behaviours and a bit more courageous to challenge in the moment. Here are some roles over my sporting career that have helped with this deeper level of awareness.

THE ATHLETE

I competed in the sporting world for over 20 years. My journey began as an Irish dancer, then as a swimmer, and later as a basketball player. Growing up in Waterford, Ireland, a city of 200,000 people, I had the opportunity to participate in various sports, always with the best support but very rarely saw women's sport on TV or had the chance to buy women's fitting kits to play in or wear as I supported my teams. As an athlete, most of my inspiration and enjoyment of sports came from the NCAA and NBA. My mam and I, in the dial-up internet days, used to sit at the computer and browse the American stores for the coolest basketball clothes and trainers.

My parents were unwavering in their encouragement (very intense at times from my father, but that was his version of support). They bought me the best dresses and curlers for Irish dancing, ensured I had the right shoes and never missed a drop-off or pick-up for the 5:30 am swim sessions. They were always there, cheering me on, and in my mam's eyes, the referee was always at fault, always there for a hug at the end of every game irrespective of the scoreline.

With such abundant opportunities, I felt fortunate to travel the world as a basketball player, representing my country and initially not recognizing the unfairness around me. I attended an all-girls school, and my basketball club had no men's teams, contributing to my early societal ignorance. However, as I grew older, travelled more and learnt, I noticed the disparities and had curiosities.

Over a 15-year period at the highest domestic and international levels, all but two of my head coaches were men. The committee members making decisions were also men, and there was a glaring absence of a player voice on critical issues. Most of the assistant coaches were men too. Of the two female coaches I encountered, one led with an autocratic style, achieving success but often through fear and intensity. The other, bringing fresh perspectives from North America, lasted only a year due to resistance from the traditional committee. I often reflect on their time as female coaches through the 1980s/1990s and who their role models were and what their journey was like.

As a player, I often felt like a pawn in a game controlled by others. We had no say in travel arrangements, accommodation, kit choices, female health support or even warm-up options for a long time. As I progressed from one of the youngest in the senior team to the captain and then an older player, I began to challenge the status quo. I became a thorn in the side of the committee, pushing for better facilities, women's-specific kits, more off-court support and, most importantly, a voice at the table.

The younger players also demanded change. Together, we slowly broke through, making incremental improvements. It was empowering to work together as a team, a group of women determined to influence the future of our club. Our breakthrough moment came when we gained representation on the committee, ensuring that the players' voices were finally heard. Former players came back to help and coach, and currently the club, with great female coaches, managers and volunteers is thriving and putting the club back on the basketball map in Ireland.

THE COACH

Looking back on my early coaching days, I cringe at the rigidity and repetition that defined my approach. As a young coach, I mimicked what I had seen from male coaches, thinking that more shouting and movement on the sidelines would yield better performance. My sister endured this embarrassing period as I attempted to transfer my energy to the young players, believing that quantity outweighed quality.

At 15, fresh from making my first national team, I fell into coaching. I replicated the styles I had experienced: regular cognitive overload, no autonomy for players and a lack of personalized coaching. It wasn't until a parent called to congratulate me on a championship win but pointed out that their dyslexic daughter struggled with my instructions that I had a wake-up call. This moment highlighted the need for a more personalized approach and made me realize how little support I had, with few female coaches to turn to.

Despite winning many games in those early years, the journey was a roller coaster, marked by sexism and ignorance. One pivotal moment was when I offered my coaching services to a school's boys' team. Despite initial success, I was dismissed in favour of a male coach who could dunk, reinforcing the gender biases prevalent in sports.

Persisting in my coaching career, I moved to coach at another all-girls school, transforming their team from the D league to national champions over four years. This experience was deeply fulfilling, as my coaching evolved, supported by the school community who valued our work regardless of gender. One of the most memorable moments was when Alan, the male PE and soccer teacher, became my assistant coach, learning and growing the sport within the school.

In my mid-20s, I transitioned to international coaching, an experience filled with highs and lows. Opportunities for women at this level were scarce, and with gratitude came sacrifices. I constantly juggled which battles to fight and which moments of inequality to address. The dismissive actions of opposition coaches and staff within my own team often made me question my path.

Speaking up for equality came at a cost. I often thought that staying silent might make life easier and secure my job while paving the way for future female coaches. However, the male-dominated coaching scene left me feeling lost and searching for belonging, ultimately leading me to step down from what I once thought was the pinnacle of my career.

Despite attempts to revive my joy for coaching in England, I felt dismissed and frustrated. Consequently, I shifted my focus to different roles across other sports, seeking to make an impact where my presence and efforts were valued.

This journey has been about more than just playing sports; it has been about fighting for fairness, equality and the right to be heard. As a woman in sports, I am proud of the progress we've made and remain committed to pushing for more.

THE ANALYST

Encouraged by my psychology lecturers, Ciara and Gerry, after completing my master's in sport psychology, I transitioned into an analyst role. They connected me with an excellent manager and team, and my analysis career flourished from there. At this point in my life, I had experienced ignorance and sexist remarks across various spaces, so when I took up the analyst role and was regularly challenged by grounds staff who mistook me for a nutritionist and wouldn't let me up to the gantry to do my work, it didn't really bother me. I had rehearsed my responses, managed my emotions and spoke assertively and politely to get where I needed to go.

This role was the first time I started working with senior men. In the dressing rooms, huddled around four or five men at halftime on a pitch or in the tunnel, feeding back relevant stats, I found myself navigating a new environment. At one point, I was one of only 2 women in a 25-person backroom staff with a GAA team, but I never felt belittled or out of place. There was no boys' club for me to break into; the managers respected me and learnt with me how we could work together. They asked how I wanted the room set up for meetings, gave me space in the training schedule and supported me in getting the players to sit, engage and listen.

However, I often found myself questioning, 'I was grateful, but should I have been?' If I were a man in this role, would I have constantly worried about fitting in, holding my own and answering questions about my role? Would I have even faced those questions about where I could do my work if I were a man? This internal dialogue was a constant companion, reminding me of the gender biases still at play.

I had to work hard and dig deep for the confidence to speak up and challenge certain decisions. It took time, and it also took a supportive mentor. Denise, who started as my boss, eventually became my mentor. She helped me thrive in this space, reminding me of my skill set when my confidence dipped, and nudging me to embrace new challenges, like becoming accredited with the Olympic Council. Denise opened her network to me, and we spent hours evolving the work I was doing, empowering me to shape the future of analysis in a country where very few women were working.

Understanding the importance of mentorship, I took it upon myself to bring interns on the journey, both men and women, to explore this role and provide the support and guidance I had received. I wanted to be the mentor that I had in Denise, helping to cultivate a new generation of analysts who could navigate this challenging field.

Despite my dedication, the stark reality of the small percentage of women in analysis, especially in GAA and football, remained. This reality often made me ponder: If there had been more women in the field, would I have stayed longer? The football obsession in England, combined with the scarcity of female analysts and the women's league not being fully professional, ultimately led me to call it a day. It was time to try on another hat, transitioning into coach development. This decision marked the next chapter in my journey, driven by a desire to foster growth and support for coaches, just as I had been mentored.

THE COACH DEVELOPER

One of the most fulfilling roles I've held, and continue to cherish, is that of a coach developer. When I moved to London, this role truly came into its own. There were ample opportunities to delve into this supportive position, and since I began in 2018, many sports, governing bodies and individual coaches have come to value the contribution of coach developers. This role resonates deeply with me because it embodies my values, offering me the chance to work closely with people, nurture delicate relationships and remain actively involved in high-performance sport, with each day presenting new challenges and rewards.

Yet, the journey hasn't always been smooth. There were threshold moments that grounded me, reminding me of the ongoing challenges women face in this field. One such moment was the call informing me that I had secured the role of coach developer with UK Coaching. I was ecstatic. I would be working with high-performance coaches across various sports, many of which I had never played. After the initial excitement of hearing about my successful interview, I paused in the staff room of the school where I was working and reflected. I almost didn't apply for the job, doubting my qualifications and abilities. My wife's encouragement and support through each stage of the interview process were crucial. At that moment, I vowed never to let self-doubt hold me back again. Apply, be brave and trust in your capabilities.

Another particularly memorable experience, but for a different reason, was meeting a coach at a café near his home. Up until this point, my gender hadn't felt like a significant issue. I knew I was one of a few female coach developers in the country, but I had successfully built relationships and learnt about various sports, preparing diligently for each interaction. However, this meeting was different. The coach, a traditionalist, greeted me with, 'Hello, love, so where have you come from (in sport)' and quickly questioned my sporting background, what I had achieved, what I knew about his sport, and eventually suggested he might prefer working with a male coach. He concluded with, 'No hard feelings, love, but I think I'd just work better with a man who's a little older with some grey hair, if you know what I mean.'

Such incidents, though not frequent, highlighted the persistent gender biases in certain sports. There isn't the visibility of many female coaches in high-performance sport, and with that comes a gap in people's ability to work, think and engage with female practitioners on a regular basis. With the scarcity of women coaching in high-performance Olympic pathways, building rapport often involved me thinking about all of these components and incorporating them into my planning for the work we might do together. It was never as bad as some other environments where I've had to think about what I wore before I went into the space and what kind of responses to have at the ready if someone was rude.

Despite these challenges, the role has been immensely rewarding. Working with high-performing coaches where gender wasn't at the forefront of people's thoughts was a testament to the progress being made. These coaches valued my expertise, showing respect and a willingness to collaborate. My approach was to be well-informed about their sport and coaching needs, show genuine care for their development and maintain strict confidentiality. This approach led to significant progress and enjoyable working relationships.

A particularly enriching experience has been my work with National Governing Bodies (NGBs), supporting their female-only programmes. While I look forward to a future where such programmes are unnecessary, I recognize their current value. These programmes and female-only conferences provide a safe space where female coaches can have their voices heard. Rugby League has done an outstanding job investing in and supporting the development of its female workforce.

Continuing to learn and develop in my field is paramount. One of the highlights of recent years has been completing my PG Diploma in Coach Development. The course, led by Bob and Andrew, provided exceptional planning and expert facilitation, making it an enjoyable and enriching experience. Their mentorship has been invaluable, helping me grow and refine my skills.

I continue to have the privilege of working with Olympic high-performance coaches who welcome me for the skillset I bring to the table, not my gender. I am passionate about encouraging women to be confident, to apply for jobs without hesitation and to support one another. We shouldn't feel grateful for opportunities that men take for granted. We deserve these roles and should seize them with confidence.

HEAD OF PERFORMANCE AND WELL-BEING

My time in professional football has been one of the most transformative experiences of my career. Working full time at a club, I found myself at the heart of an evolving space, trusted as a female leader. Navigating numerous changes, especially regarding staff dynamics and player well-being, became central to my role. Ensuring that well-being was a priority wasn't just about caring for the players but understanding that it directly impacted their performance on the pitch.

Transitioning from high-performance Olympic sports to professional football was both a leap and a refreshing change. I had heard much about the sport and had some preconceived notions about what I would face. By this point, I had moved beyond the self-doubt that once held me back and was ready to embrace new challenges. My role as head of performance and well-being for the women's first team in one of the best leagues in the world was massive and broad, encompassing various responsibilities. I created this role with the head of women's football while training to be a registered sport psychologist. Despite the presence of 25 female players, there were very few women in staff roles, making this an exploratory and trailblazing experience over three seasons.

A significant focus during my tenure was on shifting language and behaviours within the club to foster an inclusive and respectful environment. It was crucial to address how we spoke to each other, especially to women and LGBTQ+ individuals. As a gay woman, I was acutely aware of the importance of these changes. This involved having difficult conversations about female staff visibility without tokenism and carefully examining our recruitment processes, from job descriptions to interviews, to ensure women were genuinely considered for their skills and contributions. Although these changes weren't always easy, they were necessary for creating a culture where everyone felt valued and respected.

Players competing in one of the best and most competitive leagues in the world didn't need more care and attention simply because they were women. They needed people who understood female athletes' health better and saw them as individuals striving for excellence. By prioritizing their well-being and advocating for their needs, we created an environment where they could thrive both on and off the pitch.

Throughout my time at the club, I witnessed both negative language and behaviour, as well as inspiring change. We saw significant improvements: our female staff doubled, and we had signage and photos representing the great females who were part of the history of the club. We secured a women's staff changing room, women's kit, bespoke sports bras, a university partnership to support players and staff, a well-being room and fostered better relationships. These efforts culminated in a more inclusive environment through improved language and behaviour for all. I'm naming these because I'm proud of them, and with each movement came many conversations about why, how, when and who – you name it. I had support from the general manager and manager to do this work, and that made a difference. I asked the tough questions and, in some cases, asked for forgiveness rather than permission to get things moving.

As head of performance and well-being in professional women's football, I found that some people initially struggled with having a female in a leadership role, while others found it refreshing. I made it a point to lead multidisciplinary team meetings with a check-in on how people were doing first and foremost, before diving into our agenda, really trying to listen and support the person. This approach helped to build trust, cohesion and a sense of community within the team. We also had a policy that no idea was a silly idea, and nothing was off the table to discuss. If we were going to work together, all voices from interns to senior leaders were important. This took time to get used to and to become a safe space, but it was great once we got it in place.

I am particularly proud of the initiatives that doubled the female staff count and championed infrastructure improvements. My tenure at the club stands as a testament to the power of advocacy and action. It was a watershed moment of progress forged through gritted teeth, determination and collective action. It also helped when I used research to share how impactful this could be. For me, it's about the story I wanted to tell and how I wanted to leave things in a better place than I found them. At the core of it all, we are human beings, and having a person-first approach to everyday life is something we tried to do, with this came a need to look beyond gender while we challenged everyday biases.

I continue to have the privilege of working in professional sports, even though it's not at the club level, it's a very rewarding journey. It has reinforced my belief in the importance of promoting and elevating conversations on inclusivity and well-being in all aspects of sport, not only performance. The lessons learnt and the progress made serve as a foundation for ongoing efforts to create a more equitable and supportive environment for athletes and staff.

THE SPORT PSYCHOLOGIST (IN TRAINING)

I love this work; I love this journey. The biggest challenge in my role is people's fear of the unknown. Even though sports psychology has an established role in professional football, many teams are still learning to fully appreciate its value. I began this journey years ago, and now I'm in the final stages of my training in the UK, experiencing the varied standards across different countries.

As an older practitioner, I often get asked for support and guidance, and I mostly say yes so I too can learn from their journey and be that connection and support network that I needed along my journey. Sharing the journey, staying humble and learning from peers is, in my opinion, the best way to grow. The sport psychology community has been incredibly generous with their insights, time, energy and lessons over the years. Good mentoring and supervision have been crucial to my development in every role I've held, and in this field, they are essential.

My co-editor, Amy, is an inspiring force in sport psychology. Together, we emphasize the importance of diversity and global perspectives in our work. We currently work closely to look at the support needed for practitioners working in professional women's football. We know the percentage of research carried out in women's sport is so small, so this is also a way to shift the narrative and challenge beliefs around women's sport. A safe, informed working environment is what everyone across all sports deserves.

Gerry, a top sport psychologist from Ireland and co-founder of our company Impact the Game, has been a tremendous mentor and colleague in the world of performance sport. We speak about our work on a regular basis, being as inclusive and supportive as possible to coaches and practitioners across the globe. We want our work to know no gender boundaries and to have sport psychology in a relevant and digestible form for all. His humility and support have been crucial in my journey of developing as a practitioner, and he is always a glass-half-full person even when I'm sharing the toughest challenges. He has worked across women's and men's sport during his career as a successful basketball coach and consistently reminds me of the importance of sitting with the difference, challenging the norms and striving forward; don't stand still for too long.

In this field, qualifications are essential, but so is maturity. Creating boundaries and maintaining ethical standards are critical, even in intense and high-demand environments. The journey in sport psychology is a long one but very rewarding, and it is one of continuous learning and growth. I have managed to navigate these ethical dilemmas with supervision, education and confidence. Believing in the work I do and what underpins it is the best way forward. It's about fostering an environment where people feel understood and supported. It's about being part of a community that values openness and continuous improvement. Most importantly, it's about realizing that every step I take helps to break down the barriers of fear and misunderstanding surrounding psychology and well-being in sport.

Sport psychology is becoming an increasingly important part of my current work, especially as systemic shifts in women's football are happening. It's a growing role in women's professional football, and I'm proud to support the development of this field. This journey not only enhances my work but also sets the stage for my ongoing contributions to the sport.

FINAL THOUGHTS ...

Contributing to this chapter has been a journey in itself, one of reflective challenges and a great privilege. By sharing my experiences, I hope to inspire courage and reflection, urging people to think before they speak and to apologize when necessary so we can move on as we learn about each other and our own ignorance. The road ahead is long and challenging, but I am hopeful that together we can overcome obstacles and build a future where gender no longer dictates success in sports. Reflecting on my journey, I am amazed at how far I've come. Advocating for more women coaches and equitable treatment in sports has been my mission. The challenges I have faced have only strengthened my resolve.

In quite a contrasting situation, in my current role in women's professional football, I focus on performance through well-being. They accept that this is an important subject area and are investing in holistic support staff and players on their journey. Despite not having a background in playing or coaching football, my passion for positive change and advocacy for well-being and women in sport is unwavering. Our team of over 30 women working across the women's professional game comes from diverse backgrounds, and this creates a dynamic and vibrant atmosphere, fostering a supportive, productive and inclusive environment. I would urge organizations to explore their diversity and challenge their way of working to see what magic they could create.

My experiences in male-dominated coaching environments have fuelled my drive. Overcoming sexism disguised as 'banter', constant undermining and proving my worth has shaped me. Banter isn't always the best way to communicate, as it can perpetuate biases and misunderstandings. Working with Olympic high-performance coaches who value my skills, not my gender, has felt like the new normal. I am dedicated to encouraging women to confidently apply for jobs, expect more, and not accept less as we support one another. We deserve these roles and should seize them with the same confidence men do.

Let's dream of a world where every athlete, coach and practitioner – regardless of gender – can achieve success free from prejudice. I have grown through sport by moving from environments that limited me, girls to 'pink jobs' and boys to 'blue jobs', and we need to be cultivating a landscape where we are all working 'purple jobs' together. Let's continue to break down barriers and build a future where everyone, regardless of gender, can reach their full potential in the world of sports.

CHAPTER **14**
Sexisim in sport – smile more
Dr. Kristin McGinty-Minister

In this chapter we hear from Dr. Kristin McGinty-Minister who will share an insight into the latest research around women's experiences of working in sport. She will highlight her own research findings which demonstrates the need for us to hear and learn from the women's stories within this book.

GENDER INEQUALITY

Gender-based inequality, an inevitable consequence of the white, heteronormative, ableist patriarchy that has dominated society for much of human history, ensures that men possess significantly greater power, status and resources than women (e.g., Acker, 1973; Connor et al., 2016). Despite marked improvements in gender equality through policy (such as Title IX) and broader cultural change, sexism can still significantly inhibit women's progression and acts as a method of maintaining the status quo. Sexism, or discrimination or prejudice based on sex or gender, is pervasive; it is evident in laws and policies designed to control women through to our social relationships, and even our views surrounding how individuals should behave based on their assumed gender. For example, the gender pay gap in the USA has only improved by about 4% in the last two decades despite women occupying over half of the workforce (Hegewisch & Mendoza, 2023; U.S. Bureau of Labor Statistics, 2023). In the UK (and elsewhere), women suffered the brunt of the Covid-19 pandemic in terms of career disruption as a result of patriarchal drivers such as gendered social norms, preconceived notions surrounding childcare, the gender pay gap and occupational segregation (e.g., Women's Budget Group, 2021; Wielgoszewska, 2024). Outside of the economic capital women have to offer, women are encountering attacks on their autonomy on a global scale mere decades after gaining rights to make their own decisions about their finances, bodies and futures more broadly; in line with this, the United Nations believe that it will still take 286 years to close global gender gaps in legal protections for girls and women (Bergsten & Lee, 2023).

Sexism in sport

Throughout history, sport has served as a crucial factor in promoting and maintaining the current patriarchal power structure, which can be seen in the clear exclusion of women in sport throughout history (as outlined in the previous chapter; Anderson, 2009; Bourdieu, 2001). Many athletes have spoken about their experiences of being women in sport and the barriers resulting from sexism they have faced, such as a lack of maternity rights, the gender pay gap and abuse on social media (e.g., Grey & Oxley, 2024). We have witnessed the historical objectification and/or dismissal of women by the media more broadly (e.g., Trolan, 2013). While women athletes' stories have become more commonplace, the experiences and visibility of those supporting athletes are also extremely important. Women operating in stakeholder positions within sport have begun to share their experiences of gender inequity and sexism (e.g., Fink, 2016; Goldman & Gervis, 2021; McGinty-Minister et al., 2024). These stories detail an often-overlooked facet of women's exclusion in sport: how women working in sport navigate the often hypermasculine, sexist sporting environment where sexism is often brushed off as 'part of the culture'.

One major driver that contributed to my colleagues and me discussing our own experiences working in sport was the countless emerging anecdotal and academic stories from women. In communicating our own experiences and listening to those of other women, we recognized that sexism is a primary mechanism by which women might still be excluded from working in sport. For example, many women must leave their jobs in sport altogether as a result of sexist assumptions about women and motherhood (e.g., Hindman & Walker, 2020), verbal and physical abuse or intimidation (Hindman & Walker, 2020), lack of equal pay or even access to a salary (e.g., Mazerolle et al., 2017), and general gendered barriers accessing or progressing through one's sporting career (e.g., Norman, 2010). In 'Smile more: Women's experiences of sexism while working in sport', our group of researchers explored women's experiences of sexism while working in sport with the aim to gain a better picture of their experiences and see how broader and more nuanced elements of their experiences impacted them.

'SMILE MORE': WOMEN'S EXPERIENCES OF SEXISM

Introduction

105 women took the time to participate in our study by filling out a survey. When exploring these women's experiences, we used a highly reflective form of thematic analysis (Braun & Clarke, 2022) that involved using our own expertise in sport and experiences as women as valuable resources that informed how we developed the data. Through these reflective conversations, we recognized that this data had a natural fit within Bronfenbrenner's (1977) ecological model, used by Lavoi and

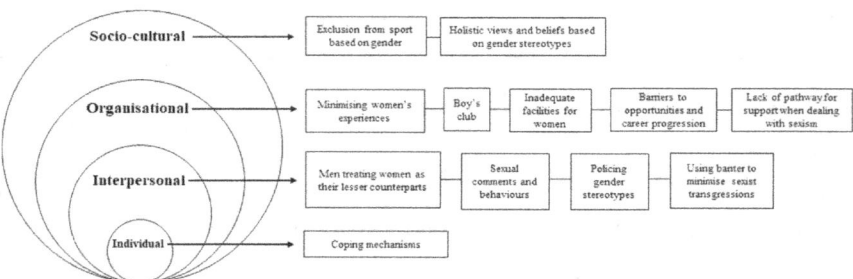

Figure 1. Overview of Themes: Women's Experiences of Sexism within the Ecological Model.

Dutove (2012) in their exploration of women coaches' experiences. With this in mind, we fit each code, evolving them into themes, into the intrapersonal, interpersonal, organizational and sociocultural levels represented in the model, which I will discuss below. Interestingly, this allows us to understand that women's experiences of sexism are a result of a complex system rather than being the fault of women themselves. A model representing our findings (Figure 1; McGinty-Minister et al., 2024) demonstrates each level of the model, but keep in mind that each level is interrelated as well. Additionally, while this chapter serves as a summary of our findings, I want to add to the depth of this by providing quotes from our participants. As emphasized by the premise of this book, women's stories are incredibly important; with this in mind, I do not want to remove participants' voices from this summary, so I have provided a table with quotes representing each subtheme (Table 14.1).

Intrapersonal (individual) experiences

At the intrapersonal, or individual, level, the ecological model considers individual factors such as psychology, emotions, interpretations, values, beliefs, biology, personal expertise and more. Think about your personal experiences and how you see and feel the world, both mentally and physically. Each woman who participated had faced sexism while working in sport. While some tried to tackle the problem head-on by

Table 14.1

Larger Theme	Subtheme	Example Quote
Intrapersonal (individual) experiences	Coping mechanism	Not many options available to you besides screaming into the void and commiserating with female friends and colleagues (emotional coping; p. 9) the reality of women's day-to-day lives in sport is very different from the reality we show. We want serious careers and that means turning a blind eye to certain behaviours (avoidant coping; p. 9).
Interpersonal sexism	Men treating women as their lesser counterparts	The group is asked a question, I answer but it's always double checked … I no longer bother answering until no one else knows the answer (p. 11).
	Sexual comments and behaviour	Told [I] was employed because [I] looked good poolside (p. 11).
	Policing gender stereotypes	Who was looking after family so they were available to attend training/gala over a weekend. Then being criticized for being away from home so much (p. 12).
	Using banter to minimize sexism	Most of the sexism I have experienced or witnessed has been brushed off as 'banter' (p. 13).
Organizational sexism	Minimizing women's experiences	Had lots of stories from my female colleagues, things like men telling women sexism does not exist in sport and that she was making it up (p. 14).
	Boys' club	The men have a 'boys' club' together and regularly meet up during the workday for coffee, go to gym, have a chat, etc. If the women do this, then we get reprimanded and branded as lazy. Important work information is discussed amongst the males in the office and is rarely discussed with the females (p. 14).

(Continued)

Table 14.1 (Continued)

Larger Theme	Subtheme	Example Quote
	Inadequate facilities for women	Inadequate facilities for female staff, etc., within workplaces (e.g. no access to women's toilets/changing) (p. 15).
	Barriers to opportunities and career progression	A colleague was overlooked for promotion. I heard the interviewing male manager say, 'She will just pop out another kid, I'm not promoting her to fund her baby making' (p. 14).
	Lack of pathway for support	Heard of derogatory comments made by a male member of staff towards both an athlete and staff members regarding physical attributes. No action was taken by the organization when this was made known to them (p. 16).
Sociocultural sexism	Exclusion from sport based on gender	I shouldn't be limiting my career options because our employment field is looking the other way when it comes to patriarchal structures within sport and exercise enacting harm – sexism affects women AND men, we owe it to everyone working in the field to do more, and do better (p. 18).
	Holistic views and beliefs about gender	I've heard men describing other men as being 'on their period' when they've displayed anger/an emotional response to something happening (p. 18).

reporting the sexism or confronting the person or people responsible, this often resulted in more sexism, which will be discussed throughout this chapter; this often meant that women engaged with different types of coping in the form of emotional or avoidant coping, which was the most common type of coping expressed by these women. Avoidant coping took many forms, ranging from 'ignoring' sexism to leaving the sporting workforce entirely, and many women avoided reporting their experiences because they feared it would damage their reputation or career. Women in sport are often pushed to adapt entirely to their surroundings to be effective and earn their place, rather than remain authentic to their respective identities and/or challenge bad behaviour. In line with this, a heavy reliance on avoidant coping styles can be a by-product of the system of sport, where women often find they need to minimize their femininity in order to be taken seriously (Champ et al., 2021; Goldman & Gervis, 2021). As will be discussed throughout this chapter, the women in our study felt they needed to use avoidant (and sometimes emotional) coping methods to keep their jobs, and sometimes even their safety, despite the potential negative consequences to their well-being.

Interpersonal sexism

Interpersonal influences arise from relationships between people such as friends, parents and colleagues; in this study, interpersonal sexism occurred from colleagues who were men and others who normalized sexism in the workplace. Being condescending towards women is a common way by which men attempt to demonstrate their dominance over women (e.g., Cooper et al., 2016), and in our study, men often treat women as their lesser counterparts. Women felt treated as inferior due to assumptions about how their gender affected their competence in the sporting workplace and described having their competence constantly doubted (e.g., Table __), often leading to avoidant coping that might impact their job performance and reinforce the false idea that women do not belong in sport. Some women described being talked down to and infantilized, while many women who consistently demonstrated their competence and did a good job despite attempts at condescension were met with intimidation tactics (such as stalking and bullying) by men. Unfortunately, women experienced consistent indirect or direct comments and behaviours that were sexual in nature; not only did women need to consider how to position themselves to be heard and able to do the jobs they were hired for, but they often needed to do this while also feeling unsafe. Women felt that they were often treated as objects rather than people, and while sexism and harassment can have an impact on performance and exclude women from sport, it is important to emphasize that no person should worry about sexual harassment, whether this be in their workplace or life more broadly.

Additionally, women discussed how others enforced gender stereotypes, expecting certain behaviours based on assumptions others made about how perceived gender impacts people's emotions, bodies, behaviours and roles. Notably, gender roles are often employed in sports to reinforce gender hierarchy; sport often assumes normative femininity in women (e.g., Goldman & Gervis, 2021), often enforcing the performance of these gender roles. For example, women were often given tasks such as making tea or doing secretarial work, which were inconsistent with their actual roles. Women are often valued only for roles that don't challenge men's power structures (e.g., motherhood and caring traits; Adams et al., 2010). When women step out of these traditional roles, they often face direct challenges about their place – one woman even lost her job because of gendered assumptions about her sexuality and promiscuity.

Additionally, banter, while not always negative, often maintains the current gender hierarchy because it disempowers the victims of sexism with its 'comical tone' (Ashburn-Nardo et al., 2014). The women in our study reported that men used banter to downplay sexism, whether it be their own sexist behaviour or that of others. Men often avoid responsibility for sexism by dismissing it as 'just banter' that is an integral part of sport culture (e.g., Nesti, 2010), making it very difficult to challenge. Participants explained how problematic banter can be, making it difficult to confront sexism. Our participants also explained that while not all banter is harmful, it can signal a lack of safety in the environment. While we are not stating that all banter is harmful, banter in sport has recently been questioned for its role in maintaining bullying and discrimination (e.g., Goldman & Gervis, 2021; McGinty-Minister et al., 2024; Newman et al., 2022). When using a 'joke' as a mechanism by which to diminish or exclude individuals or groups, banter is highly problematic and contributes to the maintenance of societal diminishment and exclusion of these groups, and clearly, can inhibit progression when attempting to call attention to the problematic nature of this speech.

Organizational sexism

While women reported significant sexism at an interpersonal level, organizational sexism, or sexism evident through organizational policies and culture, was a key perpetrator and facilitator of women's experiences of sexism. Organizational sexism excluded women by making various sporting environments difficult to access, navigate and work within through job descriptions, policies, use of space and lack of basic facilities, professional practices and more. In a world where sport has been designed by and built for men (Shaw & Frisby, 2006), the obvious and subtle organizational sexism explored by the women in our study demonstrated Fink's (2016) conceptualization of sexism as both 'overt' and 'unnoticed' in sport (p. 2).

One notable aspect of organizational sexism was the minimizing of women's experiences: women reported that their experiences of sexism and harassment were often minimized at an organizational level by excusing it as the norm, fictional or 'just banter'. Women talked about how sexism, or even sexual assault, was often either laughed off or how they were called liars when they tried to report these incidents. They mentioned how men's sexist actions were often shrugged off as 'just the way things are' or 'that's just how he is', or rebranded as harmless banter. This kind of response demonstrates why women are often forced into avoidant rather than problem-focused coping styles. Treating sexism as no big deal or integral to sport culture can impact women's willingness and ability to report their experiences, especially when many women described how addressing their negative experiences resulted in additional sexism from colleagues (e.g., being denied promotion or called a liar).

One significant method of excluding women from sporting organizations was the boys' club, or informal groups of men that acted as a method of excluding women from the groups themselves and from integrating into the organization more broadly. These groups, also known as the 'Old Boys' Club', have been historically used to exclude individuals situated outside of sport's straight, white, masculine norms (e.g., Goldman & Gervis, 2021). Alongside active exclusion from the group, this organizational mechanism of exclusion adds to the difficulty of women doing their jobs and demonstrating their competence in the workplace through being excluded from important conversations. This makes men seem more knowledgeable and women seem ineffective, only furthering the gender stereotypes that are then policed at an interpersonal level. Again demonstrating the interrelatedness between the various levels of the ecological model, the boys' club has been found to use various means (e.g., banter) to minimize and exclude women and marginalized groups, which often results in a small but dominant group of men that maintain the gender hierarchy within their own organizations and sport more broadly.

Interestingly, organizational sexism was not only evident in individuals, but also in the way sport organizations and facilities were designed, leading to inadequate facilities for women. As mentioned, sport and its respective organizations have traditionally been built for and by men and their needs (Shaw & Frisby, 2006); this includes clothing, facilities and infrastructure more broadly. This is a clear, yet often overlooked, way women are actively excluded from sport. The women in our study detailed being excluded from uniform orders and a pervasive lack of facilities such as changing rooms and access to toilets. Similar to other organizational sexism themes, a lack of basic facilities can mean women are unwilling or unable to work in these organizations, struggle to do their work to a usual standard or be met with harmful gender stereotypes that lead to further exclusion (e.g., women are picky in their clothing choices).

Unfortunately, women in our study reported that their gender was a disadvantage to opportunities for career progression at an organizational level, leading to obvious barriers to opportunities and career progression. Whether this was informal (e.g., boys' club) or illegal but commonly practised hiring practices (e.g., Table __), organizations had many ways to exclude women from progressing throughout their careers. For example, the women in our study found that they frequently experienced what is called the leadership double-bind: women who stepped outside traditional gender roles and expressed what have been considered 'masculine' leadership behaviours posed a threat within their hypermasculine environment and were met with overt acts of sexism. On the other hand, if women delivered a more 'traditional' gender performance that reflected the 'benevolent woman' stereotype, they were not seen as capable of leadership (e.g., Player et al., 2019). This common misunderstanding about what makes good leaders resulted in women experiencing significant barriers in progressing to leadership positions within their organizations.

Finally, as discussed, women struggled to report or gain support when reporting their experiences of sexism, and even harassment, meaning there was a lack of pathways for support when dealing with sexism. When asked what happened when sexism occurs within their organization, the women in our study answered that the sexism was reinterpreted, covered up by co-workers or management, that the person reporting sexism was devalued (e.g., labelled uptight or dishonest), there was outright encouragement by others (e.g., laughing or joining in), gaining support from managers to avoid negative consequences, and intimidation. In a world where a national federation accuses their star athlete of lying and threatens legal action after problematizing her assault – despite witnessing her sexual assault on a global stage minutes after winning a World Cup (Nimoni, 2023) – it is unsurprising that women who experience sexism in their own organizations might be reticent to put their career or safety, on the line by reporting experiences of sexism.

SOCIOCULTURAL SEXISM

This theme explores cultural norms and systems, such as marginalization and gender stereotypes, that impact how we think and move as a culture more broadly. As mentioned, we exist in a heteropatriarchal society where men possess even more power and privilege within sport-specific culture (e.g., Anderson, 2009). Reflecting Beard's (2017) idea that 'you cannot easily fit women into a structure that is coded as male', the women in our study felt that they were excluded from sport based on gender at a broad, cultural level (p. 86). Some women felt so unwelcome that they felt like they needed to leave sport entirely. Importantly, these hyper-masculine environments that actively exclude women (e.g., through banter, boys' clubs, and barriers to entry and career progression), therefore leading to very few visible women relative to men, maintain the idea that sport is reserved for men and that men are the primary candidates for sporting roles (e.g., Goldman & Gervis, 2021; Lafferty et al., 2022).

Overall, the intrapersonal, interpersonal and organizational levels of the ecological model are heavily influenced by the sociocultural beliefs our society/societies possess. These holistic views and beliefs about gender mean that our understanding surrounding gender stereotypes, especially in hypermasculine environments such as sport, impacts how women are viewed in an area that they deserve to operate within but was not designed for them. For example, women detailed how 'minor' comments about gender stereotypes accumulated and maintained these generalized and pervasive assumptions about gender. While unfortunately common in sport, statements like these are problematic on a number of levels. First, they maintain the idea that anything associated with being feminine or a woman more broadly is inherently negative and weak, which is often incongruent with sport culture. As a result of this, men are discouraged from engaging in normal, healthy conversation which maintains this toxic cycle that harms men as well as women (e.g., Champ et al., 2021).

THE IMPORTANCE OF WOMEN'S STORIES

Stories exploring women's experiences, though both powerful and increasing in quantity through various sources (e.g., media, books, on social media), are often disregarded on individual and broader cultural levels. The tendency to diminish women's voices as unimportant has several consequences, such as doubting the stories of survivors of assault (e.g., Epstein, 2020), reporting sexism (e.g., McGinty-Minister et al., 2024), a lack of understanding of women's bodies and healthcare needs (e.g., Criado-Perez, 2019), and a general lack of normalization of the varied experiences of women more broadly. Importantly, data from women has been excluded, ignored or actively repressed from science, literature, sport and other areas for much of history (e.g., Criado-Perez, 2019), leaving us with a very unclear picture of women's experiences and a lack of normalization of women in sport and society more broadly.

While we understand that sport is a powerful driver of social change (Kane & Maxwell, 2011) that has acted as a method of maintaining gender inequality, history has provided us with enough context to know that women's collective voices are also drivers of social change. Women have worked tirelessly on societal and sport-levels to provide us with platforms that allow us to contribute to knowledge and make the world more hospitable for women and humanity more broadly. Despite the presence of individual, interpersonal, organizational and sociocultural barriers, in recent years, the power of women's voices has created positive change in science, where we are proving that women are not small men (e.g., Thomas et al., 2020), in the MeToo movement, where women are forcing their voices to be heard (e.g., Corbett, 2023), and women athletes sticking together to protect their teammates from overt sexism (e.g., FIFPRO, 2023).

SUMMARY

In summary, our study demonstrated how women experience sexism at interpersonal, organizational and sociocultural levels within sport and touches on how women coped with their experiences at an individual level. These women's experiences support the idea that sport has historically been built for and by men, and that we must make radical changes at all levels of the ecological model to improve equity for women (and broader equity!). Ideally, this chapter has provided a framework for the reader to recognize and place some of the women's experiences in upcoming chapters. The academic work of our research team, inspired by the real stories of our lives as women working in sport and the lived experiences of the women around us, is only one piece in a larger puzzle of integrating the experiences of women in sport and making sport more accessible to those who do not currently feel welcome. On the one hand, it can be disheartening that this research leads to more questions than answers; however, questions drive change! Important questions include, 'when do I or do I not feel safe challenging sexism?' 'how can I make changes to my behaviour to make my workplace safer for those around me?' and 'which organizational changes would make the most difference to make my club more equitable?' These are important questions to reflect upon throughout the upcoming chapters when you, the reader, inevitably come across more obvious or subtle forms of sexism. I challenge you to engage with these questions, and be creative in asking new questions surrounding equity in sport – both to yourself and others!

REFERENCES

Acker, J. (1973). Women and social stratification: A case of intellectual sexism. *American Journal of Sociology, 78*(4), 936–945. https://doi.org/10.1086/225411

Adams, A., Anderson, E., & McCormack, M. 2010. Establishing and challenging masculinity: The influence of gendered discourses in organized sport. *Journal of Language and Social Psychology, 29*(3), 278–300. https://doi.org/10.1177/0261927X10368833

Anderson, E. (2008). 'I used to think women were weak': Orthodox masculinity, gender segregation, and sport. *Sociological Forum, 23*(2), 257–280. https://doi.org/10.1111/j.1573-7861.2008.00058.x

Ashburn-Nardo, L., Blanchar, J. C., Petersson, J., Morris, K. A., & Goodwin, S. A. (2014). Do you say something when it's your boss? The role of perpetrator power in orejudice confrontation. *Journal of Social Issues, 70*(4), 615–636. https://doi.org/10.1111/josi.12082

Beard, M. (2017). *Women & power: A manifesto*. Liveright Publishing Corporation, A Division of W.W. Norton & Company.

Bergsten, S., & Lee, S. A. (2023). *The global backlash against women's rights*. [online] Human Rights Watch. Retrieved from https://www.hrw.org/news/2023/03/07/global-backlash-against-womens-rights

Bourdieu, P. (2001). *Masculine domination*. Polity Press.

Bronfenbrenner, U. (1977). Toward an experimental ecology of human development. *American Psychologist*, [online] 32(7), 513–531. https://doi.org/10.1037/0003-066x.32.7.513

Champ, F., Ronkainen, N., Tod, D., Eubank, A., & Littlewood, M. (2020). A tale of three seasons: A cultural sport psychology and gender performativity approach to practitioner identity and development in professional football. *Qualitative Research in Sport, Exercise and Health*, 13(5), 1–17. https://doi.org/10.1080/2159676x.2020.1833967

Connor, R. A., Glick, P., & Fiske, S. T. (2016). Ambivalent sexism in the twenty-first century. In C. G. Sibley & F. K. Barlow (Eds.), *The Cambridge handbook of the psychology of prejudice* (pp. 295–320). Cambridge University Press.

Corbett, H. (2023). *The #MeToo movement six years later: What's changed and what's next*. [online] Forbes. Retrieved from https://www.forbes.com/sites/hollycorbett/2023/11/16/the-metoo-movement-six-years-later-whats-changed-and-whats-next/

Criado Perez, C. (2019). *Invisible women: Exposing data bias in a world designed for men*. Vintage.

Epstein, D. (2020). Discounting credibility: Doubting the stories of women survivors of sexual harassment. *SSRN Electronic Journal*, 51(2). https://doi.org/10.2139/ssrn.3575843

Fink, J. S. (2016). Hiding in plain sight: The embedded nature of sexism in sport. *Journal of Sport Management*, [online] 30(1), 1–7. https://doi.org/10.1123/jsm.2015-0278

FIFPRO. (2023). Players worldwide stand with Jennifer Hermoso. *Football Players Worldwide*. Retrieved from https://fifpro.org/en/who-we-are/what-we-do/foundations-of-work/players-worldwide-stand-with-jennifer-hermoso/

Goldman, A., & Gervis, M. (2021). Women are cancer, you shouldn't be working in sport: Sport psychologists' lived experiences of sexism in sport. *The Sport Psychologist*, 35(2), 85–96. https:// doi.org/10.1123/tsp.2020-0029

Grey, B., & Oxley, S. (2024). Elite sportswomen chasing medals on 'less than minimum wage'. *BBC Sport*. [online] 3. Retrieved from https://www.bbc.co.uk/sport/68604264

Hegewisch, A., & Mendoza, C. (2023). *Gender and racial wage gaps marginally improve in 2022 but pay equity still decades away – IWPR*. [online] Institute for Women's Policy Research. Retrieved from https://iwpr.org/gender-and-racial-wage-gaps-marginally-improve-in-2022-but-pay-equity-still-decades-away/#:~:text=In%202022%2C%20women%20working%20full

Hindman, L. C., & Walker, N. A. (2019). Sexism in professional sports: How women managers experience and survive sport organizational culture. *Journal of Sport Management*, 34(1), 1–13. https://doi.org/10.1123/jsm.2018-0331

Kane, M. J. 2011. Sex sells sex, not women's sports. So what does sell women's sports? 27 July. Retrieved from http://www.thenation.com

Lafferty, M. E., Coyle, M., Prince, H. R., & Szabadics, A. (2022). 'It's not just a man's world'–helping female sport psychologists to thrive not just survive. Lessons for supervisors, trainees, practitioners and mentors. *Sport & Exercise Psychology Review*, 17(2), 6–18. https://doi.org/10.53841/bpssepr.2022.17.2.6

LaVoi, N. M., & Dutove, J. K. (2012). Barriers and supports for female coaches: An ecological model. *Sports Coaching Review*, 1(1), 17–37. https://doi.org/10.1080/21640629.2012.695891

McGinty-Minister, K. L., Swettenham, L., Champ, F. M., & Whitehead, A. E. (2024). 'Smile more': Women's experiences of sexism while working in sport from a socio-ecological perspective. *Sport in Society*, *27*, 1–24. https://doi.org/10.1080/17430437.2024.2321357

Nesti, M. (2010). *Psychology in football: Working with elite and professional players*. Routledge.

Nimoni, F. (2023). Hermoso kiss sparks sexism debate beyond football. *BBC News*. [online] 29 August. Retrieved from https://www.bbc.co.uk/news/uk-66632652

Norman, L., Rankin-Wright, A. J., & Allison, W. (2018). 'It's a concrete ceiling; It's not even glass': Understanding tenets of organizational culture that supports the progression of women as coaches and coach developers. *Journal of Sport and Social Issues*, *42*(5), 393–414. https://doi.org/10.1177/0193723518790086

Player, A., Randsley de Moura, G., Leite, A. C., Abrams, D., & Tresh, F. (2019). Overlooked leadership potential: The preference for leadership potential in job candidates who are men vs. women. *Frontiers in Psychology*, *10*(10). https://doi.org/10.3389/fpsyg.2019.00755

Shaw, S., & Frisby, W. (2006). Can gender equity be more equitable?: Promoting an alternative frame for sport management research, education, and practice. *Journal of Sport Management*, *20*(4), 483–509. https://doi.org/10.1123/jsm.20.4.483

Thomas, G., West, M. A., Browning, M., Minto, G., Swart, M., Richardson, K., McGarrity, L., Jack, S., Grocott, M. P. W., & Levett, D. Z. H. (2020). Why women are not small men: Sex-related differences in perioperative cardiopulmonary exercise testing. *Perioperative Medicine*, *9*(1). https://doi.org/10.1186/s13741-020-00148-2

Trolan, E. J. (2013). The impact of the media on gender inequality within sport. *Procedia – Social and Behavioral Sciences*, *91*(1), 215–227. Retrieved from https://www.sciencedirect.com/science/article/pii/S1877042813025512

UK Women's Budget Group. (2021). Women and employment in the recovery from Covid-19. *Autumn budget 2021 pre-Budget briefings*. Retrieved from https://wbg.org.uk/wp-content/uploads/2021/10/Employment-Autumn-2021-PBB-1.pdf

U.S. Bureau of Labor Statistics. (2023). *Labor force participation rate for women highest in the district of columbia in 2022: The economics daily: U.S. bureau of labor statistics*. Retrieved from https://www.bls.gov/opub/ted/2023/labor-force-participation-rate-for-women-highest-in-the-district-of-columbia-in-2022.htm#:~:text=For%20the%20nation%20as%20a

Wielgoszewska, B. (2024). *The gender furlough gap: Why did women stop working at higher rates than men? – Data Impact blog*. Retrieved from https://blog.ukdataservice.ac.uk/the-gender-furlough-gap/ [Accessed 25 July 2024].

CHAPTER **15**
The ripple effect – the power of inspiring stories

Jen Coe, Dr. Amy Whitehead, and
Dr. Kristin McGinty-Minister

As discussed in the introductory chapter of this book, there are endless ways of maintaining gender inequity, with sport being one major mechanism for doing so. We outlined that not only have women been excluded from sport, but sport has played a large, historical role in slowing progress towards gender equity more broadly. Women's steadfast courage and progress have resulted in an inevitable backlash such as sexism and leveraging powerful men to encourage women to retain their more traditional gender roles. However, we see this backlash for what it is: today's bicycle face and imposter syndrome. The women outline their stories, detailing how, sometimes without recognizing these hurdles for what they were at the time, gendered barriers influenced their journeys. As readers, we gain insight into courageous accounts of breaking down cultural and societal barriers as coaches, athletes, scholars and activists; how imposter syndrome still acts as a barrier to women in prominent roles in sport; the importance of relying on other women for support, respect, encouragement and confidence in a culture that often tries to deny individuals such things; the importance of (and obstacles surrounding) challenging stereotypes in hypermasculine cultures; how being courageous enough to take the right opportunities at the right time can positively impact one's life and career – and many more inspiring stories.

It is important to note that these stories are not just for women: there is a great deal of wisdom and courage to be found for any reader. Yet, as inspiring as these stories are, it is the hope that they will also challenge you, the reader. We hope the opening questions in the introduction how stayed with and continue to support next steps 'have you questioned how to be an 'ally' to those around you, or how to improve your organizational practices to progress gender equity? On how and why sport and gender inequity are so linked? In this final chapter, we explore how to progress gender equity in sport by discussing the various roles of women, other individuals and sport organizations and continue to challenge readers to reflect upon the questions posed as well as the thoughts and emotions that might arise.

OVERCOMING GENDER INEQUITY IN SPORT

Importantly, in this section exploring potential ways to progress gender equity, we continue with the theme of decentralizing the issue of gender equity in sport; gender inequity is not a problem caused by women, and women and allies have worked tirelessly throughout history to overcome the barriers presented by patriarchy Additionally, many modern women have been told that they can accomplish their wildest dreams since they were children, despite pervasive ignorance of the many hurdles that accompany women's lives (and despite some thinking this is a 'diabolical lie'); as a group, (most) women have acted accordingly, whether their dream was to be a homemaker, veterinarian or own a sports franchise. However, many men have not been taught how to be unlike the men who came before them and progress alongside women. Therefore, while we begin by emphasizing the importance of women continuing to tell their stories, we continue this section by outlining how men and other individuals can become educated allies who actively challenge gender inequity. Following this, we explore how organizations, which bear significant power and responsibility in the sporting world, can make changes to improve gender equity. At the end of each section, we provide some reflective questions to initiate reflective practice and provide the opportunity for the reader to challenge themselves.

WOMEN – KEEP STORYTELLING!

Note that the odd, women-specific 'inflictions' discussed in chapter 1 of this book (e.g., bicycle face, women's perceived incapacity for team sports) often served the purpose of limiting the gathering and communication of women. Just as the historical perception of women speaking to one another as 'gossip' in order to problematize (and sometimes demonize) their active communication, women's stories, especially women with intersecting marginalized identities, have had their stories actively repressed for centuries (e.g., Federici, 2019; hooks, 1981; Veenstra, 2019). This has led to significant hurdles such as gaslighting in important areas such as medicine (Khan et al., 2024), harassment (Epstein, 2020), sexism (e.g., McGinty-Minister et al., 2024) and more. While on one hand this is frustrating, there is an important lesson we can derive from this: women's stories are powerful. Why would patriarchal systems minimize or silence women's stories if they were not compelling and meaningful?

When our research team (McGinty-Minister et al., 2024), having separately experienced various forms of sexism but not knowing how to navigate this, used the tools at our disposal (our modern bicycle: Microsoft Teams) to share our stories, we recognized the importance of raising awareness of these experiences. We appreciated the significance of talking about our own small and large experiences, those of our colleagues and friends, those of other academics and women throughout the world (e.g., the MeToo movement). Women consistently experience gender inequity but have a difficult time sharing their experiences because of systems designed to defend patriarchy, such as sexism. Not only is each individual's story important, but continuing to tell our stories can be healing and contribute to knowledge surrounding women and their lives. Stories have long driven change in sport, and as a result, society; women have the power to drive this change by employing the expertise of their own lives and vocations, as evidenced by the stories throughout this book.

In line with this, women should lean on one another in friendship and mentorship. Relying on the built-in support system often offered by other women, despite being 'looked down upon' by patriarchal standards, can provide significant support in one's well-being, development, and career more broadly. Women are often the biggest champions of other women, and by combining the power of telling our stories and creating connections, we have the chance to accelerate our development as individuals, practitioners and in sport more broadly. With this in mind, we do not wish to offer 'tips' in this chapter for managing gender equity, further placing the burden on women (and marginalized genders more broadly); rather, it is important for women to lean more into themselves and one another, tell their stories, share and persevere as people grow and learn. In line with this, we ask the reader to think about *what groups they are part of: women, do you have a supportive group of women around you (personally or at work)* that might have gone unnoticed at this point? Organizations – *what do you see in the pattern of relationships being built in your space?* Important questions like these can provide a depth of information about where to seek support, inspiration and information.

BE AN EDUCATED ALLY

While the word 'ally' has had an important role in identifying non (or less) marginalized individuals supporting and taking action towards progress, we hope to soon move beyond that word; allyship should be the minimum qualifier in relationships, where the alternative is actively contributing towards inequity.

Importantly, one primary driver for change is an understanding of oneself and the world; from my perspective, individuals, regardless of sex or gender identity, have the responsibility to educate themselves about the world they live in. Men and other allies must become aware of how their actions and the actions of others can contribute to gender inequity. For example, in sports, interpersonal sexism (e.g., banter, condescension) is incredibly common and poses significant barriers to women attempting to operate within the sporting context (e.g., McGinty-Minister et al., 2024). Individuals should take active ownership of their education rather than placing the educational burden on surrounding marginalized groups.

Alongside this, men should utilize the privilege offered by sport culture to minimize sexism in their respective environments. In sport, which is often run by men and for men, women often struggle to question or dispute gender inequity – especially since this has the chance to negatively impact their job security or physical safety (e.g., McGinty-Minister et al., 2024). Even men who witness sexism and are aware that it is problematic are unlikely to challenge or question sexism, especially if this is perpetrated by an individual with power; unfortunately, men are more likely to engage in sexism in these situations (Ashburn-Nardo et al., 2014). This often leads to the perpetuation of sexism within the environment, more barriers to reporting or calling out sexism and obvious active exclusion of women. However, unlike the consequences women face when challenging sexism, men are often listened to when they dispute or question sexist behaviours around them (e.g., Drury & Kaiser, 2014). With this in mind, men have the ability and responsibility to challenge sexism, gender inequity and other prejudices when they recognize it. Men, we encourage you to engage in reflective conversations with friends and colleagues who are men when the chance arises and to challenge sexism (and gender inequity more broadly) head-on where possible. In fact, consider the format of the groups around you – are you surrounded by many similar people, or do you have a diversity of opinions and experiences around you (and why might this be the case)? Additionally, without placing an educational burden on women, speak to women (friends, family, colleagues) about their experiences – their stories. Ask what support looks like for them, and how you might provide this. Finally, engage in individual reflection on your own behaviours and biases in the workplace and beyond. Some important questions to consider are:

1. Who have you relied on for education on topics surrounding equity?
2. What does your privilege look like in the context of your life?
3. Have you weaponized your privilege or used your privilege for progress (whether intentionally or unintentionally)?
4. Am I someone a woman can rely on for support, and what does this look like?
5. Do I participate in potentially harmful interpersonal sexism (e.g., banter)?

SPORT ORGANIZATIONS

Broadly speaking, sport organizations possess significant responsibility in problematizing and mitigating gender inequity and sexism in sport culture. Importantly, this does not diffuse responsibility from individual men: sport organizations are often run by men, and therefore, the responsibilities discussed above still apply. For example, recent research in the UK has demonstrated that only 53% of professional sport clubs have a woman on their board, none of which have a woman in a leadership position; across all Olympic national governing bodies, an average of 34% of women comprise boards, while on professional teams, only 8% of board positions are held by women (Farrer & Co, 2019). These statistics represent professional organizations managed with carefully designed policies, and women's representation is likely worse in non-elite or non-professional sport. Individuals in leadership positions, ranging from grassroots to professional levels, must employ education and allyship to implement organization-wide changes that can impact those working within their respective organizations and sport culture more broadly, and as a result, society (e.g., Kane & Maxwell, 2011). One way to accomplish this is through providing education on gender, gender equity and sexism to stakeholders and athletes. An individual must be able to recognize sexism in order to interpret it as problematic, and being able to perceive sexism in the workplace offers the opportunity for individuals to change their interpretations and behaviour and challenge problematic behaviours and policies. Organizations can accomplish this by hiring consultants and outside experts to provide scientifically backed, culturally relevant education and applicable plans of action, goals and monitoring and evaluation.

While education is an integral step in challenging sexism, organizations have significant work to do in terms of addressing their patriarchal design and subsequent execution of gender inequity through policy and culture. For example, while having children often leads to less pay for mothers, men with children earn significantly more – earning more income than both men and women without children. In the US, fathers experience a 21% wage increase upon becoming a father, while women experience an 11% motherhood penalty in wages; resumes from fathers score higher than identical resumes from non-fathers, while resumes from mothers score the lowest (BBC, 2016). In Denmark, having a child has been found to contribute to 80% of the gender wage gap (e.g., Kleven et al., 2018). A significant reason for this motherhood wage gap can be attributed to patriarchal standards and values that filter through to organizational practices (e.g., attitudes towards working men and women, and assumptions about who takes on caring responsibilities). In sport, women have described a double standard (e.g., standards for professional practice), and others have outlined how women often have to work twice as hard as men to access or maintain their space in sport (e.g., needing to be perfect while men are often given the benefit of the doubt when making mistakes). Applying equity throughout various organizational levels, whether this be through tolerance of problematic behaviour from employees, hiring and promotion practices, access to basic facilities such as toilets or equitable pay, is an essential step in improving gender equity.

In line with this, equitable hiring practices can expand the number and visibility of women role models in general stakeholder and leadership positions. Whilst many fear that women in positions of power might detract from the care of men, recent research has confirmed what feminists have been declaring for decades, rather than 'hating men, feminisms strives for gender equity to make living better for everyone and feminists cared about men more than any other group cared about men (Hopkins-doyle et al., 2024). More women (and marginalized groups more broadly) involved in sports can lead to positive impacts such as the normalization of varied ways of living and leadership styles, different perspectives that can lead to improved performance providing men and boys with women role models and, importantly, providing women and girls with role models that represent broader pathways to success situated outside historically prescribed gender roles (Madsen, 2015; Turban et al., 2019).

While it is all well and good to intend to improve equity in opportunity and the visibility of women role models, intent is not enough in the sporting world, which is currently ingrained within and perpetuates patriarchal norms. Importantly, organizations must begin this work by changing policy to be inclusive and facilitative of everyone's development, for example, implement consequences for sexist behaviour; it is imperative to change the support pathways for women to report inappropriate behaviour so that these consequences have meaning. Implement quotas or change hiring practices so that pervasive bias less significantly impacts who is hired. However, it is important to reflect upon how to do this: even 'blind' orchestra auditions are not immune to gender bias, with the smallest detail (the sound of 'women's' shoes on the stage floor) influencing hiring practices (e.g., Goldin & Rouse, 2000). Fight against the aforementioned contributors to the gender pay gap and inequality more broadly by designing a policy that allows women within an organization to progress through clear pathways, equitable pay and access to basic rights such as maternity leave and pay. In line with this, all individuals should have maternity/paternity leave and pay: caregivers are not purely women. For example, gay couples who decide to have children and work in sport (and beyond) likely struggle to take leave to support the development of their children. Additionally, men married to women who have children are also involved in contributing to the development of their children and household, and lack of paternity leave often contributes to the innumerable barriers to women remaining and progressing in the workforce (e.g., Kleven et al., 2018).

While these changes are by no means easy, they are imperative in creating a more equitable environment that allows space for individuals situated outside the patriarchal power structure that drives sport. In doing so, sport organizations can reflect the progression of society and also improve their performance, as diversity is significantly related to performance in organizational environments (e.g., Carruci, 2024). Additionally, countless stories of athletes and stakeholders (e.g., Champ et al., 2021; McGinty-Minister et al., 2023) illustrate the negative impact the hypermasculine culture of sport has on well-being; beginning to dismantle patriarchy within one's organization can address this. In order to create this positive change, organizations can hire various professionals as consultants, or better, integrate these individuals within their organizations to advise on relevant changes and see them through to execution. Importantly, organizations should ensure they are listening to the women within and outside of their organizations. In doing so, sport organizations have the opportunity to significantly impact individual lives and sport culture more broadly, and as a result, can be a driver of change in society. Some key questions organizations should ask themselves include:

1. What are my values, and is the functioning within the organization reflecting these?
2. Are individuals and groups within the organization educated on gender inequity and what this looks like in practice (e.g., what sexism is)?
3. How do this organization's policies contribute to women's inequity in sport?
4. What kind of policies do we have in place that promote equity?
5. How can we better include women in organizational decision-making?

SUMMARY

In summary, we have progressed to where we are today with gender equity because of the power of brave women and their stories. The power of these stories is evident in the inspiring, motivating and educational accounts shared by the women throughout this book and beyond. Women, keep telling your stories, regardless of whether you perceive their significance to be large or small. Importantly, rely on and support other women. Outside of that, it is essential to decentralize gender inequity and sexism; just as Reshma Saujani (Chapter 2 of *Brave, Not Perfect, 2019*) describes how imposter syndrome is not truly a women's issue, the problem of gender inequity should primarily be addressed by men, allies, organizations and society more broadly. We implore individuals to become more reflective about their own thoughts and biases and how they impact the world, and equally, how cultural systems impact the world around them. For example, how do you currently perpetuate or fight against gender inequity? Organizations have the responsibility and ability, through their privilege, to create progressive change in sport.

As discussed, sport has the potential to directly impact the direction of society more broadly. Historically, sport has been designed and maintained to perpetuate patriarchy, using the key instrument of repressing women from sharing their stories through the active barring of women from sport and cultural manipulation (e.g., bicycle face). In chapter 1 of this book, we challenged the reader to consider whether sexism is integral to sport culture. After sharing some historical context, learning about how women experience sexism while working in sport, and a book full of inspiring stories from women in sport, we understand that gender inequity is (and has always been) innate to sport culture. We have explored why that is and have offered some exploration into what we might do about it – but there is still a great deal to be done. Having answered those questions, we have one more question for you, the reader, to consider: bearing in mind the precipice of change we now occupy and the significant influence of sport on society, how can we use sport to dismantle rather than maintain patriarchy?

REFERENCES

Ashburn-Nardo, L., Blanchar, J.C., Petersson, J., Morris, K.A. and Goodwin, S.A. (2014). Do you say something when it's your boss? The role of perpetrator power in prejudice confrontation. Journal of Social Issues, 70(4), 615–636. https://doi.org/10.1111/josi.12082.

BBC. (April 25, 2016). Working fathers get 21% 'wage bonus', TUC study suggests. BBC News. [Online]. Available at: https://www.bbc.co.uk/news/business-36126584 [accessed July 26, 2024].

Carucci, R. (2024). One more time: Why diversity leads to better team performance. Forbes. [Online]. Available at: https://www.forbes.com/sites/roncarucci/2024/01/24/one-more-time-why-diversity-leads-to-better-team-performance/#.

Champ, F., Ronkainen, N., Tod, D., Eubank, A., & Littlewood, M. (2020). A tale of three seasons: a cultural sport psychology and gender performativity approach to practitioner identity and development in professional football. Qualitative Research in Sport, Exercise and Health, 13(5), 1–17. https://doi.org/10.1080/2159676x.2020.1833967.

Drury, B.J., & Kaiser, C.R. (2014). Allies against sexism: The role of men in confronting sexism. Journal of Social Issues, 70(4), 637–652. https://doi.org/10.1111/josi.12083.

Epstein, D. (2020). Discounting credibility: Doubting the stories of women survivors of sexual harassment. SSRN Electronic Journal, 51(2). https://doi.org/10.2139/ssrn.3575843.

Farrer & Co., (2019). Women in Sport - Report - Page 1. Farrer & Co Women in Sport - Report - Page 1. [Online]. Available at: https://www.paperturn-view.com/uk

/briannawilson/farrer-co-women-in-sport?pid=NzA70913&v=1.1 [accessed November 8, 2022].

Federici, S. (2019). How the demonization of 'gossip' is used to break women's solidarity. In These Times. [Online]. Available at: https://inthesetimes.com/article/the-subversive-feminist-power-of-gossip.

Goldin, C., & Rouse, C. (2000). Orchestrating impartiality: The impact of 'Blind' auditions on female musicians. American Economic Review, 90(4), 715–741. [Online]. https://doi.org/10.1257/aer.90.4.715.

Grady, C. (2020). Some say the Me Too movement has gone too far. The Harvey Weinstein verdict proves that's false. Vox. [Online]. Available at: https://www.vox.com/culture/2020/2/24/21150966/harvey-weinstein-rape-conviction-sexual-predatory-assault-me-too-too-far.

Hooks, B. (1981). Ain't I a Woman: Black Women and Feminism. New York: Routledge.

Hopkins-Doyle, A., Petterson, A. L., Leach, S., et al., (2024). The misandry myth: An inaccurate stereotype about feminists' attitudes toward men. Psychology of Women Quarterly, 48(1), 8–37.

Kane, M.J., & Maxwell, H.D. (2011). Expanding the boundaries of sport media research: Using critical theory to explore consumer responses to representations of women's sports. Journal of Sport Management, 25(3), 202–216. https://doi.org/10.1123/jsm.25.3.202.

Khan, K., Tariq, N. ul S., & Majeed, S. (2024). Psychological impact of medical gaslighting on women: A systematic review. Journal of Professional & Applied Psychology, 5(1), 110–125. [Online]. https://doi.org/10.52053/jpap.v5i1.249.

Kleven, H., Landais, C., & Søgaard, Jakob Egholt. (2018). Children and gender inequality: evidence from Denmark. National Bureau of Economic Research Working Paper Series. [Online]. Available at: https://www.nber.org/papers/w24219.

Madsen, S. (2015). Why do we need more women leaders in higher education? HERS Research Brief, 1, 1–8. [Online]. Available at: https://digitalcommons.usu.edu/marketing_facpub/157/ [accessed September 7, 2022].

McGinty-Minister, K.L., Swettenham, L., Champ, F.M., & Whitehead, A.E. (2024). 'Smile more': women's experiences of sexism while working in sport from a socio-ecological perspective. Sport in Society, 1–24. https://doi.org/10.1080/17430437.2024.2321357.

Rice, S., Oliffe, J., Seidler, Z., Borschmann, R., Pirkis, J., Reavley, N., & Patton, G. (2021). Gender norms and the mental health of boys and young men. The Lancet Public Health, 6(8), e541–e542. [Online]. https://doi.org/10.1016/S2468-2667(21)00138-9.

Turban, S., Wu, D., & Zhang, L. (2019). Research: When gender diversity makes firms more productive. Harvard Business Review. [Online]. Available at: https://hbr.org/2019/02/research-when-gender-diversity-makes-firms-more-productive.

Veenstra, G. (2019). Race, gender, class, and sexual orientation: Intersecting axes of inequality and self-rated health in Canada. International Journal for Equity in Health, 10(1), 1–11. [Online]. https://doi.org/10.1186/1475-9276-10-3.